Great Sacred Music

Great Sacred Music

*A resource book for
mission through music*

Samuel Wells
Andrew Earis

Canterbury
Press

© Samuel Wells and Andrew Earis 2025

Published in 2025 by Canterbury Press
Editorial office
3rd Floor, Invicta House,
110 Golden Lane,
London EC1Y 0TG, UK
www.canterburypress.co.uk

Canterbury Press is an imprint of Hymns Ancient & Modern Ltd
(a registered charity)

Hymns Ancient & Modern® is a registered trademark of
Hymns Ancient & Modern Ltd
13A Hellesdon Park Road, Norwich,
Norfolk NR6 5DR, UK

All rights reserved. No part of this publication may be reproduced,
stored in a retrieval system, or transmitted,
in any form or by any means, electronic, mechanical,
photocopying or otherwise, without the prior permission of
the publisher, Canterbury Press.

The Authors have asserted their right under the Copyright, Designs and
Patents Act 1988 to be identified as the Authors of this Work

British Library Cataloguing in Publication data

A catalogue record for this book is available
from the British Library

ISBN: 978-1-78622-573-3

Typeset by Regent Typesetting
Printed and bound by
CPI Group (UK) Ltd

CONTENTS

Preface — vii

Introduction — 1

Seasons — 9

Advent — 9
Christmas — 11
Epiphany — 15
Candlemas — 18
A journey into Lent — 20
The Annunciation — 23
Holy Week — 25
Easter — 28
Ascension — 31
Pentecost — 33
Harvest — 36
All Saints — 38
All Souls — 41
Remembrance — 43

Hymnwriters — 46

George Herbert — 46
John Donne — 48
Richard Crashaw — 50
Isaac Watts — 53
William Blake — 55
Cecil Frances Alexander — 57
John Henry Newman — 59
Gerard Manley Hopkins — 62
Robert Bridges — 64
Contemporary hymnwriters — 66

Saints — 69

Michael	69
St Francis of Assisi	72
St Luke	74
St Cecilia	76

Occasions — 79

New Year	79
Valentine's Day (14 February)	81
Sea Sunday (July)	83
Anniversary of the coronation of King Charles III (6 May)	86
World Water Day (22 March)	88
International Day of Peace (21 September)	90
World Space Week (4–10 October)	93

Choral Works — 95

Allegri's Miserere	95
Vivaldi's Gloria	98
Handel's *The Messiah*	100
Mozart's Requiem	103
Haydn's *The Creation*	105

Hope — 108

And I saw a new heaven	108
Lord of all hopefulness: Lord of all joy	110
Lord of all hopefulness: Lord of all faith	112
Lord of all hopefulness: Lord of all grace	115
Lord of all hopefulness: Lord of all calm	117

Faith — 120

The Word of the Lord	120
The Lord's my Shepherd	122
Justice	125
Prayer	127
I want Jesus to walk with me	129
O for the wings of a dove	132
Blessings	134

PREFACE

This is a book that describes an event that has taken place at St Martin-in-the-Fields in London every Thursday, barring Covid, since 2013, and online, regardless of Covid, for much of that time. It also describes an experience made possible by a host of dedicated and talented people, musicians, staff and volunteers, and shared by many people faithfully and regularly, and countless people occasionally and curiously. But its real purpose is to begin a movement that changes the way people approach sacred choral music, the way people think about making faith accessible to seekers and the lapsed, and the way people think about what church really is.

It originates in the two authors finding in each other and, in the everyday miracle that is St Martin-in-the-Fields, fertile ground for experimentation in beauty, discovery and hope. Those who have become doyens, if not addicts, of Great Sacred Music over the years have, we believe, done so because they too have relished that beauty, shared that discovery and found that hope.

Among those many colleagues who have made this all possible, we are especially grateful to those who have prepared, conducted, accompanied and organized, with particular thanks to organists Polina Sosnina, Ben Giddens, Jeremy Cole, Richard Moore and Nicholas Wearne, and current and past members of the music management and administration team including Alicia Hill, Phoebe Palmer, Isabelle Palmer, Cathy Martin, Sarah Maxted, Alice Usher and Helen Freudenberg. Other colleagues and volunteers, too many to mention, have nonetheless provided the shoulders on which this wonderful tradition has sat.

The book is dedicated to all who have sung with St Martin's Voices at Great Sacred Music since it began in November 2013, and who have, thereby, made many hearts sing.

*For all who have sung with St Martin's Voices
at Great Sacred Music*

INTRODUCTION

This is a book designed to be used in one of two ways. The first is that churches may wish to hold events at which they can invite those of faith or no faith to enjoy beautiful singing, sung to a good standard (or played on a recording), explore and discover some of the theological, historical and musical background to the music, and reflect on a range of themes of general or specialized interest. This book gives suggestions of suitable themes, appropriate music of different levels of demand, and scripts that may be used to amplify the spoken parts of the event. The second way the book may well come to be used is for a house group or small gathering – to be posh it might be called a soirée – that could play recorded music (or perhaps employ a piano to accompany the hymns) and use the scripts for educational and devotional purposes rather than aesthetic ones. Each script is intended as a lifting-off point to stimulate ideas and provoke reflections. This introduction offers more detail behind what this book seeks to offer.

Words and music

Soon after I came as vicar to St Martin-in-the-Fields in 2012 I stumbled upon an impasse. We had lunchtime concerts three days a week and a Choral Eucharist one day. That left Thursdays. The clergy were leading some creative and thoughtful events – but no one was coming. So I made a suggestion. I recalled my time in North Carolina 2005–12, and a radio station rather like Classic FM. It offered an intriguing programme on a Sunday morning with a billing I couldn't forget: 'Did you know [spoken in the broadest Southern drawl] that much of the great classical music that we enjoy today has *religious* origins?' The question was asked so insistently and so ingenuously that all I could ever think was, 'Well I never!' The programme was called *Great Sacred Music*.

So I thought, hilariously uneducated as the question was – maybe it was onto something. That something was the large overlapping space between enjoyment of classical music and appreciation of Christianity. Just as an art appreciation class thrillingly explains all the symbols and motifs in a Renaissance painting, so one could have a comparable experience if someone were to explain a hymn or a choral anthem and identify the points of interest or surprising twists that make the piece stand out. But unlike a painting, with a piece of music there is an opportunity to join in – together. There could be a mix of choral anthems sung by a choir, and hymns in which all those present joined. But it mustn't be a worship service – we already had plenty of those; instead, it must be all the bits of worship that a visitor or returner would find most attractive and least threatening. The point would be that someone attending could hold it at arm's length – yet be so moved by the music, or provoked by the explanations, that they experienced something like worship without needing to call it that.

The draw is the music: what's not to like about beautiful music adeptly sung? But along with appropriate publicity and a warm welcome, the other dimension is the nature of the spoken elements. The stance I chose to adopt from the beginning in November 2013 was that of the wry observer. In other words, expressly not the pious presider, leading people into prayer and devotion, nor the concert host, talking up the performers and pieces, nor the teacher, communicating information with style and an eye for detail. Instead, I've continued to build a relationship with those attending (we don't use the terms audience or congregation) through eschewing comprehensiveness or reverence, and seeking instead to evoke curiosity, engage scepticism, and employ humour. I set myself the aim of saying something sufficiently interesting for those attending to be eager to pass on its flavour to whoever they have dinner with that evening. I'm always looking for a point of surprise, which provokes a reaction of 'Well, how about that?' And when it comes to the theological parts, my aim is to come at them askew: for example, to say that Protestants always tend to think of Mary as basically a Catholic, or that Ascension is a test-case of whether theology really has got beyond a notion of heaven 'up there' and hell 'down there'. I'm not trying to sell those attending anything, nor turn the event into a worship service on the sly by adding a prayer or becoming homiletic; I'm trusting the elements of the event to combine hospitality, humour and beauty in ways that speak for themselves.

We had to create a professional choir for the event, which we did by inviting our choral scholars and alumni to participate: this became St Martin's Voices, now a choral music phenomenon, whose members still see Great Sacred Music as their core activity. We had to generate funds to cover our costs: we decided on a retiring collection rather than ticket sales. In inviting donations, we ask people to invest in a movement, rather than simply pay for an event. We needed to generate a handout, with two hymns on the inside pages, a running order and credits on the front, and an opportunity to advertise on the back. And in due course we've added what our culture has made possible: livestreaming, contactless giving, and advertising on social media. Today, around 200 people attend every Thursday, with another 20,000 watching online in the course of a month. We have replicated Great Sacred Music events around Britain and in the USA. And we have a sister programme, Choral Classics, on a Sunday afternoon. Our numbers in the building dropped 20% post-Covid due to office workers working from home – but our online following grew by a far greater proportion. After ten years, we decided it was time to create a resource that could encourage others to adapt and apply these principles to their own context.

Faith and no faith

Twenty years ago, I wrote a book called *Improvisation: The Drama of Christian Ethics* (Grand Rapids, MI: Brazos and London: SPCK, 2004; second edition Grand Rapids, MI: Baker 2018). The central argument of the book is that the scriptural story shows a God who, when faced with adversity, does not block, by resisting, nor accept, by succumbing, but *overaccepts* by fitting things into a larger story. Thus, most obviously, Jesus neither blocks the cross nor accepts the cross but, in the Resurrection, over-accepts the cross. Great Sacred Music was, in its inception, an attempt to mimic the work of the Holy Spirit by not blocking the public's appetite for classical music, nor simply accepting it, but over-accepting it and enabling people to perceive how it fits into a larger story. It has become one of the most evident of many such examples of over-accepting at St Martin's in recent years.

The ethos behind Great Sacred Music, its beauty, its humour and its studied understatement, is a theology of the Holy Spirit. If you are anxious about the scarcity of God, and tacitly assume God cannot function unless we strain every sinew to introduce God into every space and time, then all becomes preaching, and preaching becomes the transmission of key information about God to a third party as explicitly as possible, with specific measures of what counts as success – measures such as church attendance, financial giving, holiness of life, commitment to evangelism, and (sometimes) social or political engagement. By contrast, if you trust in the abundance of God, in the conviction that the Holy Spirit has been at work in your life since your life began, and that the Holy Spirit makes Christ present not just in the Church but in a whole variety of places to the widest diversity of people, then ministry takes on a different character. Ministry becomes a matter of creating the right kind of environment where the Holy Spirit can reasonably be relied upon to show up. That 'reasonable reliance' is based on the church's historical and contemporary experience. Beauty, truth and goodness are descriptions of spheres in which the Holy Spirit has invariably been experienced. Healthcare and education have long been forms of service in which the Church has assumed that the Holy Spirit's work of transformation and enlivening comes about every day.

The approach taken at Great Sacred Music is the latter one. This is for a number of reasons. First, St Martin's is in the centre of London: a lot of visitors, many of them tourists, but a good many with a half hour to kill between meetings or museum or theatre visits, pass by, and persuading some of them to stop to eat, or listen, or pray, is a daily challenge and opportunity. Some are looking for something they know and trust – and terms like Evensong or Choral Eucharist assure them they know what they're coming to. Others are looking for something different: they're prepared to give music a try, and a free event in a central London landmark is worth a look. Others again have serious reasons not to want to enter a church: many have experienced congregational life as controlling or narrow, or an occasion for rejection or hurt; yet many such people still yearn, still love, still search – and the secret to their hearts is not an uncompromising message but a gentle overture. A second reason is that we're not communicating a message – we're sharing a love. It's a love that's hard to describe. It might be simply that we enjoy the sound of choral singing. It might be that we've been shaped significantly by the choral tradition – we perhaps sang in an ensemble in our youth, or went to a school that had a choral liturgical rhythm, or attended a church with a fine choir – and haven't been part of something like that for a while. It may be that we've enjoyed choral music on the radio, or attended some concerts and kept the tunes in our head long after. It may be that we have significant instrumental experience, but less knowledge or understanding of church. Or it may be that we've watched *Songs of Praise*, or are familiar with hymn singing, and have felt somewhat inadequate about our ignorance as to choral or classical music in general, and are glad for an entry-level invitation to observe and enjoy. Whatever the reason, something short (35 minutes), accessible (everything is subtly explained), regular (every Thursday so you can come once or frequently) and not too serious is an easy invitation to accept.

A decent test is that, not knowing what to say, around half the attendees say thank you for the service, while another half say thank you for the concert. When we did a survey, we found a third came for the music, a third for the spoken parts, and a third for the combination – which we felt was about right. One church official said it was the best form of evangelism he'd seen in years; but the secret is, we don't call it evangelism, and we don't think about it intentionally as a subtle way for people to find or rediscover faith or church. Instead, we set out to have fun. The Voices sing magnificent sixteenth-century choral music but also throwaway closing numbers from musicals or popular culture. I talk about the difference between pain and suffering and why African American spirituals focus so much on rivers, but I also find salacious stories about who was having an affair with whom when he wrote a wedding anthem for somebody's daughter. One person said, 'You've introduced me to a kinder Christianity': the intention is to respect those attending in their multifarious encounters with God, faith and church, and simply provide an environment where they can think, laugh, reflect, listen – and, if they desire and are so moved, pray.

Congregation and choir

I don't robe for Great Sacred Music – though I do wear a clerical collar; but we do have two hymns – which I introduce by saying, 'We remain seated while the Voices stand and lead us.' While for regular churchgoers it can feel natural to stand for hymns and confusing not to, the whole sitting-standing-kneeling routine can be bewildering for visitors and less than conducive to relaxed concentration. We sing hymns at Great Sacred Music for a number of reasons. The first is, it's not a concert. There's a good deal of very rewarding listening to do, but that's not the whole of what we're about: there are things for us to do together too. The second is, hymns are the single most accessible and most direct form of conventional worship most people experience. As Augustine famously says, 'The one who sings, prays twice' – in word and in song. The third is, elementary crowd psychology tells you that if people have actively participated in word or deed in an event within the first ten minutes it changes how they feel about being there. It's obviously absurd for 200 people to go round the room introducing themselves, but singing a hymn engages a different part of body and brain in much the same way. Singing a hymn at the equivalent point before the end rounds off the experience in a similarly satisfying manner. Not everyone sings – whether because they struggle with the language, can't keep up with the tune, have no voice, or don't feel comfortable with the faith dimension of the words: but that's fine – this isn't a test of people's commitment; it's an additional outlet and expression for their enjoyment.

There are generally five, sometimes six, choral works. We've tried in this book to emphasize the range of these – in genre, authorship, provenance and historical era. We seldom feel a need to cover every angle in a single event: the point is subtly to challenge notions. There are many such notions that need challenging: most obviously that classical music is a white bourgeois domain, but also that all composers are men, that all 'real' music was composed before the eighteenth century, that music that originated in secular settings has nothing to offer to the choral liturgical tradition, or that contemporary praise music or African American spirituals or musical theatre are somehow beneath trained choirs. This book traverses the world, enjoys folk and modern worship songs, dips into oratorios and challenges itself to respond to secular festivals. It's not variety for its own sake – it's seeking to model a new normal for a culture – choral music – that, like many others, could make the mistake of associating the way it's always been done with the way it ideally should be.

Expertise and enthusiasm

The way we've done Great Sacred Music at St Martin-in-the-Fields is more professional than many churches would wish to or be able to imitate: we have the opportunity to attract talented singers early in their careers in a context where there are enough other singing opportunities available that they can hope to make a living performing with us and elsewhere. At the same time, we are in a thriving cultural centre with 450 ticketed events per year and six or seven sung services per week and around a million visitors through the door: the expectation is of a high standard of performance and our business plan relies on putting on events for which people are prepared to pay.

This is obviously not everyone's context. This book is absolutely not saying that everywhere needs to be like St Martin's. But it absolutely is saying that we have found a programme of this kind, blending choral and congregational singing with light-touch commentary and an unthreatening welcome, has immeasurably enhanced the enjoyment and understanding of regulars, attracted and kept many who might have found the threshold of attending a Sunday or weekday worship service too daunting, and offered a way to promote a culture around music appreciation that doesn't take itself too seriously yet is a memorable aesthetic, educational and devotional experience.

These things are perfectly possible in other social and ecclesial contexts. Let's imagine you have a lively tradition of visiting the churches of one another's denominations in a market town during the Week of Prayer for Christian Unity; an interdenominational choir could practise suitable pieces and there could be four or five events that transcend the difficulties presented by ecumenical worship. Or if you have a pattern of a Lent course, you could take the five great choral works offered in this book, and perhaps invite a choir months in advance to perform them. The key is to see what's possible, and not succumb to the 'if only' or 'we can't do that' or 'it's all right for some' mentality. A church must strive to be what only it can be, not be a failed version of somewhere else. Perhaps your community has got used to online community during Covid and kept up that practice since: maybe you could do a series based on this book that works for people as an online event.

The music for this book has been chosen based on the repertoire that we perform each week at Great Sacred Music. The difficulty level varies from simple to complex, but the focus is always on how the choice of choral music serves the theme. The vast majority of music choices should be achievable with a reasonably good mixed-voice choir. We encourage those using this book to treat each script as a lifting-off point to stimulate ideas, and to adapt repertoire to suit the choral forces available.

The last thing this book would want to do is suggest that unless you have outstanding singers and an established theologian you can't do Great Sacred Music. We're presenting the book not as a definitive canon of what constitutes a brand, but as a provocation, a resource and an invitation to the reader to replicate such events in a local context, with local resources, and, often with some forward planning and imagination, limitless possibilities. The overall experience of Great Sacred Music should be one of joy – joy in making music, joy in discovery, joy in laughter, understanding, insight and surprise, joy in learning, joy in aesthetic admiration, joy in finding and being found by God.

Structure and sources

Each script in the book bar one (Christmas) has the same structure. We experimented for the first few months in 2013–14, but since we landed on this structure, we've never altered it, except once a year for the Five Lessons and Carols just before Christmas. We begin with a choral anthem – we've found it compelling to go straight into music and capture the imagination from the start. I don't say anything about the opening piece – indeed I avoid commenting on anything retrospectively: all the remarks are about things we're about to hear or sing, including the final remarks before the closing anthem. The spoken introduction has three components: a brief welcome, a theological overview of the theme, and an introduction to the first hymn. After the hymn we present three anthems. In these scripts I have introduced all three together. In practice I seldom do that, because it's too much spoken word (and subsequently too much music) at one go; in addition, often the accompanist has to make the long journey between organ and piano. Then after the third anthem I introduce the second hymn. Finally, I invite a donation, advertise any upcoming events, and introduce the final anthem, which often has a throwaway or surprise character to it. At the end those attending always applaud – and I join them clapping as an appreciative member of the gathering rather than bowing as a performer: the point is, the whole of my contribution is to enhance the appreciation of all gathered of the music we hear and sing, so I clap to express that appreciation on my own part. I don't greet people at the back like a clergyperson after a service; but I do loiter at the front, where people invariably come and want to talk about the music or something I've said.

I make no pretence at being a musician, let alone a musicologist. A neck injury acquired on the rugby field aged 20 put an end to my singing talents, which were very limited to begin with. I've never learned to play an instrument, because it was all sport for me as a child and I've been too stubborn since. Part of the joy of Great Sacred Music has been my own joy – joy at learning so much about so many different composers, hymnwriters, extraordinary stories and remarkable coincidences. There are few things more thrilling than passing on exciting news you've just learned yourself.

In putting together the scripts in this book, I have relied heavily on three sources especially. J. R. Watson, *An Annotated Anthology of Hymns* (Oxford: Oxford

University Press, 2002), is a simply outstanding book that has been my chief companion for the last ten years of presenting Great Sacred Music. In addition, Frank Colquhoun, *A Hymn Companion: Insight into 300 Christian Hymns* (London: Hodder and Stoughton, 1985), has offered a very helpful alternative source, especially for Free Church hymns for which Watson did not find space. Though considering a smaller selection, Ian Bradley, *The Daily Telegraph Book of Hymns* (London: Continuum, 2005), is also a treasury of wisdom and research. It's hard to imagine Great Sacred Music without these three sources. For other information, I have shamelessly scoured the internet for countless parish notes, composers' blogs and dictionary summaries. I take little credit for any of the brief introductions, many of which are compiled from various of the above sources to whom the chief credit should go. I haven't interrupted the scripts with tiresome and repetitive footnotes, but it's important I don't claim an authority that doesn't rightly belong to me. By contrast, the theological overviews and periodic interjections are my own. I always joke that Great Sacred Music is about Andrew and the Voices giving me a musical education and me giving Andrew and the Voices a theological education: perhaps the fact that we're all still learning is what gives it its energy and joy.

After each piece of music, the published sources are listed. This is not an exhaustive list, and in many cases there is more than one publisher for a particular work. Where a piece is out of copyright, this is listed as public domain, and can be found on websites including the Choral Public Domain Library (CPDL) and International Music Score Library Project (IMSLP). Sometimes, a public domain piece also has a well-known published edition, sometimes found in a volume widely used by choirs: for example, *The Oxford Book of Tudor Anthems* or *European Sacred Music*, in which case this is listed too.

Our hope is that this book will prove the catalyst for your community to discover, explore and inhabit the extraordinary (and to some, new) realization that much of the great classical music that we enjoy today has religious origins – and that taking this realization further will be a profound blessing to you, as it has been to us.

SEASONS

Advent

Choir: 'Jesus Christ the apple tree' – Elizabeth Poston (Banks Music Publications)

Advent

- This is the season when we recognize the tension between what has been revealed, Jesus' first coming as a baby in Bethlehem, and what has yet to be revealed, Jesus' second coming in clouds of glory. The word 'advent' means coming, so it refers to both the first and the second coming. One Advent tradition is to assign to each of the four Sundays of Advent the four last things – Death, Judgement, Heaven and Hell – although these days, reflecting on hell a mere 48 hours before Christmas has gone rather out of fashion.

'O come, O come, Emmanuel'

- Fifteen hundred years ago, the early monks marked the seven days leading up to Christmas Eve, assigning to each day one of the scriptural names of Jesus – wisdom, Lord, root of Jesse, key of David, Morning Star, king of all peoples, and Emmanuel, God with us. Put together in Latin, the first letter of each title spells Sarcore. Read backwards, Sarcore reads Ero Cras, which means 'I will be here tomorrow.' So the resultant hymn is a secret code that contains the whole of Christmas – Jesus' coming – and the whole of Advent – the hope of his second coming.
- In the thirteenth century, a Latin monk made five of the antiphons into a hymn and added the chorus. The hymn was translated by J. M. Neale in 1851 into the form we know it today.

Hymn: 'O come, O come, Emmanuel' (Veni Emmanuel)

Three anthems

- 'E'en so Lord Jesus, quickly come' was written in 1953 by Paul Manz with lyrics adapted from the book of Revelation by Ruth Manz. It was written during a

time when their three-year-old son was critically ill. Their son did recover, which the couple attributed to the prayer.
- 'A spotless rose' was probably written in German in the sixteenth century, and was first published in 1599. It emphasizes the royal genealogy of Jesus, and its theme is the first verse of Isaiah chapter 11, 'And there shall come forth a rod out of the stem of Jesse, and a Branch shall grow out of his roots.' Jesse was the father of David, from whose line the Messiah was expected; but that line is depicted as a tree stump, because kingship had been interrupted in Judah since the exile, five centuries before the coming of Christ. The second verse explains that Mary is the spotless rose that has sprung forth, the spotlessness referring to her virginity. It's a curious reference, since Jesus' genealogy in the Gospels is traced through Joseph rather than Mary.
- 'A tender shoot' is also a setting of Isaiah 11, one of the passages traditionally read at a service of Nine Lessons and Carols. As in the previous piece, the imagery is saying that David's line, the monarchy, was sliced across and thus ended like a tree cut off at the base of its trunk at the exile when Judah was taken into Babylon in the sixth century BCE; but that a descendant of David would nonetheless take up his mantle. Christians have always read this passage as pointing to Jesus. Kerensa Briggs is an emerging composer, raised in choirs in Gloucester and at Kings College London, whose music has been described by the *New York Times* as 'poignant, ambivalent, and quietly devastating'.

Choir: 'E'en so Lord Jesus, quickly come' – Paul Manz (MorningStar/Oxford University Press, *Advent for Choirs*)
Choir: 'A spotless rose' – Becky McGlade (OUP)
Choir: 'A tender shoot' – Kerensa Briggs (Boosey & Hawkes)

'Long ago, prophets knew'

- Gustav Holst arranged a tune called '*Personent Hodie*' from an original sixteenth-century melody known as '*Piae Cantiones*'. Fred Pratt Green was approached to write an Advent hymn to go with it. The writing is vigorous – it's bold to rhyme 'knew' with 'Jew' – and the chorus of bellringing conveys the theme of preparation and anticipation. The second verse echoes the words of Galatians 4.4, 'when the fullness of time had come'. The third verse brings us to the threshold of Bethlehem.
- This is very much Advent understood as preparation for Christmas, rather than anticipation of Christ's coming again.

Hymn: 'Long ago, prophets knew' (Personent Hodie)

'People, look East'

- This hymn was written by Eleanor Farjeon (1881–1965) in 1928. Farjeon, a native of London, was a devout Catholic who viewed her faith as 'a progression toward which her spiritual life moved rather than a conversion experience'. She achieved acclaim as an author of children's nursery rhymes and singing games, and is best remembered for her poem 'Morning has broken'. She declined a damehood explaining that she 'did not wish to become different from the milkman'.
- East is the direction of the rising sun and, in the history of Christianity, the direction of the coming Messiah. In the second verse, the bare earth is waiting for the seed that will flourish in the reign of the Promised One. In the third verse, the stars that guided the Magi shape the 'bowl' of the heavens, giving signs of hope beyond 'the frosty weather'. The angels' song, in the fourth verse, sets 'every peak and valley humming', an oblique reference to Isaiah 40.4: 'Every valley shall be exalted and every mountain and hill brought low …' The poem defines Love as 'Guest', 'Rose', 'Bird', 'Star' and 'Lord'.
- Christopher Steel was a British composer whose work, including seven symphonies, has been compared to Walton and Britten. He died on his 53rd birthday in 1991.

Choir: 'People, look East' – Christopher Steel (Banks Music Publications)

Christmas

Unlike other scripts, this one follows the pattern of Five Lessons and Carols.

Christmas and carols

- The incarnation is the central doctrine in Christian theology, from which all other doctrines flow. The person whom the disciples recognized as God among them, who became the Saviour who brought God's purposes to a climax, was identified with the Creator who had shaped his life to be for humanity from the very beginning, and became the source of the Holy Spirit who empowered the life of the Church. Søren Kierkegaard offers a parable to clarify the nature and purpose of the incarnation. A king fell in love with a humble maiden. He considered how he might woo her. If he were to court her with the trappings of majesty, she might love him for the wrong reasons. Yet if he were to dress up as a person of her own class, her love, if it came, would be founded on deceit.

Thus he must become a person of her own class if he were genuine in his desire to win her heart. For Kierkegaard, the idea that Jesus only seemed to be a human being but was really a veiled form of God all along, an idea known as Docetism, misses the point entirely. But Kierkegaard goes almost too far the other way, and seems to suggest Jesus lost his divinity in becoming one of us.

- From the beginning, the early Church affirmed that there was still only one God. The fact that Jesus had been both God and human did not mean either that there were two gods or that Christ was simply a temporary mode of God's existence and thus that heaven was empty while Jesus walked on earth until he ascended and returned. The doctrine of the Trinity emerged as theologians articulated that God fully lived in Jesus, but when Jesus died, God did not cease to be. Meanwhile, Jesus, while undoubtedly God, was just as much a human being. Between the fourth and seventh centuries, discussion raged among theologians of East and West over how Jesus could have a human nature and will, and also a divine nature and will, while still being one person, rather than two. The Chalcedonian Definition of 451 preserved this understanding of Christ. It said Jesus was truly and fully human, fully and truly divine, yet remained one person.

- There have always been challenges to the Chalcedonian understanding of who Jesus is. The most pressing contemporary challenge is from a feminist perspective. How important is it that, when God took human form, that form was male? If Jesus was fully human, and yet a man, does that mean that women are an insignificant or derivative aspect of 'full humanity'? If, as many early theologians asserted, 'the unassumed is the unhealed', can a male Saviour save women? For much of the Church's history, the maleness of Christ was taken for granted by many as essential to the character of his divinity. This view is much less common today, and the character of Jesus' full humanity is more often found in his complete trust in God and his identification with the most estranged and excluded groups in society.

- In the Middle Ages, carols were circle dances associated with festivals or mystery plays. They went out of fashion during the Reformation out of Calvinist distrust of folk and Catholic revelry. Carols were revived by modern songwriters, like George Ratcliffe Woodward, the author of 'Ding Dong merrily on high'; and most of all by Edward Benson, Bishop of Truro and later Archbishop of Canterbury, who created the service of Nine Lessons and Carols in 1880, which was taken up in 1918 by Eric Milner-White at King's College, Cambridge.

- Today carol services are often accompanied by candles, mince pies and mulled wine; the irony is that these outdoor forms of celebration are closer to Bethlehem, and to the medieval notion of a carol, than the more formal ceremonies inside churches.

'Once in royal David's city'

- This hymn was written by C. F. Alexander to correspond with the words in the Apostles' Creed, 'born of the Virgin Mary'. It tells the story as a children's tale, beginning 'Once', as all good such stories do. The story ends with our becoming like stars around God's throne. Sarah MacDonald is a Canadian musician who is Fellow and Director of Music at Selwyn College, Cambridge, and Director of the girl choristers at Ely Cathedral.

Hymn: 'Once in royal David's city' – arr. Sarah MacDonald (*Carols for our Time*, Encore Publications)

1st lesson: Isaiah 9 – Christ's birth and kingdom are foretold by Isaiah

'The Oxen'

- Thomas Hardy's elegiac poem 'The Oxen' is a classic demise-of-innocence account of the nativity. It is based on the myth that the animals in the stable knelt for the birth of Jesus – and that animals today kneel accordingly at midnight on Christmas Eve. Disillusioned, Hardy says, 'So fair a fancy few would weave / In these years!' – but he can't deny he would still join others in hope should a crowd go to find out for themselves. It's a powerfully contemporary poem of disillusionment and mystery, despite being over a century old. Jessica French is a contemporary composer of choral works based in Seattle.

Choir: 'The Oxen' – Jessica French (OUP)

2nd lesson: Luke 1 – The Angel Gabriel salutes the Blessed Virgin Mary

'Angelus ad virginem'

- This is a thirteenth-century Latin carol, which shaped a Basque folk carol, which was paraphrased by the late nineteenth-century Anglican priest Sabine Baring-Gould, who had spent a winter as a boy in the Basque country. The paraphrase is 'The angel Gabriel from heaven came'. The Latin version was originally an acrostic, where the initial letters of the 27 verses of the song spelt out the alphabet. It is mentioned in Geoffrey Chaucer's 'The Miller's Tale', written around 1390. Carol Barnett is a mid-western composer of choral music, musical theatre and opera.

Choir: *Angelus ad virginem* – arr. Carol Barnett (OUP)

3rd lesson: Luke 2 – St Luke tells of the birth of Jesus

'Away in a manger'

- Contrary to popular opinion, this carol is not by Martin Luther. It appeared in the USA in 1885, originally with two verses, eventually with three. Its secret is its precise focus on the mystery of infinity concentrated in this tiny creature, and on the love the baby stirs in child and adult alike. Lucy Walker is composer-in-residence with St Martin's Voices at St Martin-in-the-Fields.

Choir: 'Away in a manger' – Lucy Walker (Boosey & Hawkes)

4th lesson: Luke 2 – The shepherds go to the manger

Wexford Carol

- The Wexford Carol is of unknown origin, but its style suggests it was composed in the fifteenth or sixteenth century. It came to be known as the Wexford Carol because the organist and musical director at St Aidan's Cathedral in Enniscorthy, County Wexford, in the south-western corner of Ireland, William Grattan Flood (1859–1928), transcribed it and entered it in the *Oxford Book of Carols*, published in 1928 and edited by Percy Dearmer, Martin Shaw and Ralph Vaughan Williams. The carol tells the familiar story of how Joseph and Mary looked in vain for a place to stay; there are two verses about the shepherds and a final one about the wise men. Sarah Quartel is a contemporary Canadian composer and educator.

Choir: Wexford Carol – Irish trad. arr. Sarah Quartel (OUP)

5th lesson: John 1 – The incarnation of the Word of God

'Hark! The herald-angels sing'

- The first line of this Christmas hymn was originally 'Hark! How all the welkin rings' – where welkin means heaven (or heavens); the hymn was one of a set of five in the same metre, the others marking Epiphany, Easter, Ascension and Pentecost. The original hymn had ten four-line stanzas and a much greater emphasis on Jesus' role in reversing the Fall. The words were changed by George Whitefield and the verse structure by Martin Madan. The familiar tune was adapted from a chorus in Mendelssohn's *Festgesang*, a work composed in Leipzig in 1840 to celebrate the anniversary of the printing press. Mendelssohn thought the tune too slight for a serious hymn. The tune required a repetition of the first two lines as a refrain.

Hymn: 'Hark! The herald-angels sing' – arr. Sarah MacDonald (*Carols for our Time*, Encore Publications)

'All and some'

- 'All and some' is an anonymous fifteenth-century text, written in the macaronic style. Macaronic weaves phrases of liturgical Latin with vernacular Middle English. It is a lively invitation to join joyfully together to celebrate the bliss of salvation disclosed in Christ's birth. The irresistible, dance-like triple metre draws the listener in as an active participant in the carol, emphasizing the inclusive and invitational message of the text. Olivia Sparkhall is a conductor and composer and author of *A Young Person's Guide to Vocal Health*.

Choir: 'All and some' – Olivia Sparkhall (Banks Music Publications)

Epiphany

Choir: 'Eastern monarchs, sages three' – June Nixon (Encore Publications)

Epiphany

- 'Epiphany' means appearing, showing or revelation. It focuses on the story of the magi coming from afar to worship the baby Jesus. The story of the star represents the way God reveals the truth of all things not just to Jews but to Gentiles. The story has shaped the way Christians think about other faiths, represented by the magi themselves, and about science, represented by the magi's sighting the star. In both cases, with science and other faiths, the story shows how our wisdom can get us to Jerusalem; but only revelation, represented in the story by the chief priests and scribes searching the Scriptures and finding a line in the prophet Micah, can get us that short extra step from Jerusalem to Bethlehem, from the palace to the stable.
- Epiphany names a season of such revealings, including Jesus' first miracle, turning water into wine at Cana, an event that sums up John's Gospel in its transition from the water of life to the wine of eternal life. There is also the call of the first disciples and Jesus' sermon in his hometown synagogue. In various ways the disciples and the Church today try to comprehend the wonder that is before us – just as the magi did when they came to the stable.

'As with gladness men of old'

- William Chatterton Dix was a true son of Bristol, whose second name honours the Bristolian poet Thomas Chatterton (who died aged 17); Dix attended Bristol Grammar School, where I was to follow in his footsteps 125 years later. He became manager of a maritime insurance company in Glasgow, where he spent most of his life. He was an Anglo-Catholic who wrote a great number of hymns, and had a passion for versifying translations of ancient Greek and Abyssinian hymns. Many of his hymns, including 'As with gladness men of old', were written in his bed at the age of 29 after he suffered a near-fatal illness and months of depression. Among his other hymns are 'Alleluia, sing to Jesus', and the harvest hymn 'To thee, O Lord our hearts we raise'. The irony of 'As with gladness men of old' is that its German tune is named 'Dix' in its author's honour, even though he is known not to have liked it.
- 'As with gladness men of old' was published just in time to be included in the first edition of *Hymns Ancient & Modern* in 1861. The hymn comes in two parts. Part One includes the first three verses, which each adopt the structure 'As they …' and 'so may we …' The first verse is about being led to God; the second, reinterpreting the manger as the mercy-seat in the Jerusalem Temple where Jews sought reconciliation with God, is about finding forgiveness in Christ; the third is about laying all our costliest treasures at God's feet, just as the magi did. Part Two leaves the traditional Epiphany story behind. So verse 4 turns attention to the day of judgement, praying that we may be brought into God's presence at a time and place where no star is any longer needed to guide us. Finally, verse 5 remains in the heavenly realms, uniting our praise and the magi's faithful searching with the glory of the angels singing God's glory for ever. It's the only well-known Epiphany hymn or carol about the visitors from the east that avoids referring to them as either magi or kings and doesn't state how many there were.

Hymn: 'As with gladness men of old' (Dix)

Three anthems

- One November morning in 1983, the young organist and composer Paul Edwards gathered up his week's pile of laundry and was about to leave for the local launderette when he found a letter from the poet Paul Wigmore. In the launderette he loaded the machine, read the poem, grabbed a scrap of manuscript paper and wrote this carol, 'No small wonder'. It was first performed in the service of Nine Lessons and Carols at King's College, Cambridge in 2000.
- In 1916, Herbert Howells was diagnosed with Graves' disease and given only a short time to live. Radium injections were largely successful in providing a cure, but left the composer weak. In his convalescence he wrote 'Here is the little

door' as part of a set of three, published 1918–20. The text is a tender poem by Frances Chesterton, wife of the poet and writer G. K. Chesterton. In the poem, gold is for a king, incense represents prayer and myrrh means death. The poem suggests the gifts were genuinely for the baby.
- Bob Chilcott tells of the glory of the star of Bethlehem with a translation of two verses by French hymnwriter Charles Coffin, augmented by a new verse from Chilcott's long-time collaborator Charles Bennett. The carol both tells a story and dwells upon it, blending traditional and contemporary themes. Charles Coffin was an eighteenth-century rector of the University of Paris, now known as the Sorbonne. He wrote many hymns, mostly in Latin, several of which were translated and published by John Henry Newman in 1838. He was a Jansenist, being part of a movement in the Catholic Church encompassing Jean Racine and Blaise Pascal that identified with the doctrine of grace as set out by Augustine. Jansenism drew close to Calvinism in its low view of free will and its high view of justification by faith.

Choir: 'No small wonder' – Paul Edwards (*Christmas in Blue*, Boosey & Hawkes)
Choir: 'Here is the little door' – Herbert Howells (Stainer & Bell)
Choir: 'Epiphany' – Bob Chilcott (OUP)

'O worship the Lord in the beauty of holiness'

- John Monsell was an Ulsterman, whose father was Archdeacon of Derry, who studied at Trinity College, Dublin, being ordained in 1834. His eldest son died in a shipwreck on the way to the Crimean War, and his daughter also died in her twenties. After serving in the Church of Ireland for 20 years, he was called to be Vicar of Egham in Surrey and subsequently St Nicolas' Guildford. He had a penchant for restoring churches, at Ballycastle, Egham and Guildford, but the habit was to prove his downfall, as while at Guildford in 1875 he fell from the church and died from an infected wound. Monsell published 300 hymns, of which the only ones widely sung today are 'O worship the Lord in the beauty of holiness' and 'Fight the good fight with all thy might'. He came from a muscular school that believed hymns should be ardent and joyful. He published his hymns in the 1873 volume *The Parish Year*. In 'O worship the Lord in the beauty of holiness' he composed one of the greatest hymns in the language, constituting a whole theology of worship, based around two of the three gifts of the magi, gold and frankincense.
- The opening line of the hymn comes from Psalms 29 and 96 and 1 Chronicles 16. The hymn is soaked in scriptural references: the burden of carefulness comes from Philippians 4, which speaks of our anxiety, while the slenderness of our wealth recalls the widow's mite. The mornings of joy and evenings of tearfulness are derived from Psalm 30 and the verse 'weeping may endure for a night but joy

comes in the morning'. The hymn never fully leaves the stable setting of the first verse and the devoted offering of the gold and frankincense. The second verse contrasts our lowliness and God's greatness, and speaks of three contexts for intercession – comforting our sorrows, answering our petitions and guiding our actions. The third verse describes how truth and love are more worthy signs of worship than money. The fourth verse reminds us that all prayers heard in Jesus' name will reach the Father. The repetition of the last verse affirms the cycle of worship that never ends.

- Monsell's pastoral skill is epitomized in the understanding of the three principal occasions for prayer named in the three central verses: discernment (guiding thy steps as may best for thee be), stewardship (these are the offerings to lay on his shrine) and help (trust for our trembling and hope for our fear).

Hymn: 'O worship the Lord in the beauty of holiness' (Was lebet)

'Follow that star'

- Peter Gritton was Director of Music at James Allen's Girls' School in London. His humorous piece still conveys the significance of the four journeys of Christmas – that of Joseph and Mary to the stable, of the shepherds from the fields, of the magi from eastern lands afar, and most of all of Jesus from heaven to earth. Epiphany epitomizes the way all these journeys are part of the revelation that is Christmas.

Choir: 'Follow that star' – Peter Gritton (Chester Music)

Candlemas

Choir: O nata lux – Thomas Tallis (words and melody public domain, published in *The Oxford Book of Tudor Anthems*, OUP)

Candlemas

- Candlemas is the popular name for the feast of the Presentation of Christ in the Temple, which according to Luke's Gospel took place 40 days after Jesus' birth. Before you complain that Matthew has the visit of the wise men and the Holy Family hotfooting it to Egypt by then, the truth is there's no use trying to reconcile Matthew's chronology with Luke's.

- Once Joseph and Mary reach the Temple, they're greeted by Simeon and Anna, both ancient of days, and together representing the hopes of Israel. As elsewhere, Luke presents male and female together here, with a similar contrast between the ancient ones and the infant Christ.
- Note that the Temple is where the first story of Luke's Gospel is set, and the Temple is where the last two stories of Luke's prologue take place – this one and the discussion between Jesus aged 13 and the doctors of the law when he'd eluded his parents' grasp.
- John Ellerton was a nineteenth-century vicar and hymn compiler. He wrote 'The day thou gavest, Lord, is ended'. This hymn was written in 1880, for Mrs Brock's *Children's Hymn Book*.

Hymn: 'Hail to the Lord who comes' (Old 120th)

Three anthems

- 'When to the temple Mary went' was written by Johannes Eccard who lived from 1533 to 1611. He was a German Protestant contemporary of William Byrd. The words were added by John Troutbeck 300 years later. Troutbeck also made the accepted translations of the St Matthew and the St John Passion.
- The Nunc dimittis is the song in which Simeon, who has spent his whole life in the Temple, finally sees salvation in the form of the baby Jesus. The anthem juxtaposes the end of one life with the beginning of life for all. It offers a very positive view of old age. Gustav Holst wrote this anthem in 1915. He was passionate about Byrd's music – shown clearly here in his modal writing and the way the male and female voices answer one another.
- Of the many resonances of light in the Old and New Testaments, one of the most abiding is the metaphor of the Holy Spirit lighting our path through good times and bad. It's a constant theme of the psalms, and this composition by Brad Nix, a Baptist based in Texas, combines Jewish and Christian understandings of salvation – and rhythm. Look out for a spectacular conclusion.

Choir: 'When to the temple Mary went' – Johannes Eccard (public domain)
Choir: Nunc dimittis – Gustav Holst (Novello)
Choir: 'The Lord is my light' – Brad Nix (Hal Leonard)

'Christ whose glory fills the skies'

- This hymn was published by Charles Wesley in 1740. It was inspired by the Benedictus – the song of Zechariah in Luke 1 that speaks of the tender mercy of God from whom the dayspring from on high has visited us.

- The hymn balances the inspiration of dawn with the analogy of spiritual light. It echoes the Wesleyan emphasis of inner light overcoming the darkness of sin.
- The German tune 'Ratisbon' (the oldest town in Bavaria) dates back to before Luther, but this 1815 tune was used in the 1861 edition of *Hymns Ancient & Modern*.

Hymn: 'Christ whose glory fills the skies' (Ratisbon)

'This little light of mine'

- By the time of his early death at 45 from a brain tumour, Moses Hogan was considered the world's greatest arranger of spiritual music. He published 88 vocal arrangements. He was born in New Orleans and grew up in a choir led by his uncle. He was also an accomplished painter.
- 'This little light of mine' emerged in the 1920s. It was not originally a spiritual. It eventually became a Civil Rights anthem in the 1950s and 1960s. It concluded Meghan and Harry's wedding in 2018.

Choir: 'This little light of mine' – Trad. spiritual arr. Moses Hogan (Hal Leonard)

A journey into Lent

Choir: *Miserere mei* – William Byrd (words and melody public domain, published in *The Oxford Book of Tudor Anthems*, OUP)

Theme

- Lent begins on Ash Wednesday, six and a half weeks before Easter, and provides a 40-day period for fasting and abstinence (Sundays don't count), in imitation of Jesus Christ's fasting in the wilderness before he began his public ministry. The period also echoes Israel's 40 years in the wilderness before entering the Promised Land. A period of penitential preparation for baptism (and those seeking restoration after egregious sin) was first formalized at the Council of Nicaea in 325 CE. Sackcloth and the sprinkling with ashes evidenced their penance. This form of public penance began to die out in the ninth century. The practice of receiving ashes on the disciple's forehead on the first day of Lent gradually saw Lent becoming a devotional period for all, rather than just those preparing for baptism.

- Today the practices of Lent include self-examination, prayer, fasting, alms-giving, Scripture reading and the repair of broken relationships. Lent traditionally has a 'half-way' point on the fourth Sunday, marked in the UK as Mothering Sunday; thereafter the mood moves from personal piety to a focus on Jesus' path to the cross.

'Forty days and forty nights'

- There can be few better matches of tune and words than the seventeenth-century Heinlein with 'Forty days and forty nights'. The minor chords vividly point to Christ's struggle with Satan. We discern not only Christ's wilderness, but our own voluntary and involuntary wilderness. We stretch all our muscles for greater readiness, like a long jumper getting closer to the ground before the final great leap. Fasting is about taking away the excess, so our bodies belong wholly to God. Eventually the hymn issues into the joy of Easter and the struggle is over.

Hymn: 'Forty days and forty nights' (Aus der Tiefe)

Three anthems

- Tomás Luis de Victoria (1548–1611) was a Spanish composer and contemporary of Giovanni Pierluigi da Palestrina among the principal composers of the late Renaissance. He was a Catholic priest, as well as an accomplished organist and singer, and he worked in Italy as well as Spain. His *Officium Defunctorum* is considered one of the great sacred choral music compositions of the Renaissance and takes several elements of the Requiem Mass. It was composed for the funeral of Maria, wife of Holy Roman Emperor Maximilian II.
- The Portuguese Vicente Lusitano was the first Black composer to have his music published. He was born in Olivença, then a Portuguese city (now in south-west Spain), around 1520. This was a time when almost all Black people in Europe were slaves. It's not known how he gained his musical education, but in 1551 he published *Liber primus epigramatum*, a collection of 23 motets. By 1561 he had married and become a Protestant. *Emendemus in melius* is a text often sung at the imposition of ashes on Ash Wednesday. It goes: 'Let us amend for the better in those things in which we have sinned through ignorance; lest suddenly overtaken by the day of death, we seek space for repentance, and be not able to find it.'
- 'Wash me throughly' is a setting of Psalm 51 by S. S. Wesley. Psalm 51 is the definitive penitential psalm, recalling David's affair with Bathsheba and his search for redemption thereafter.

Choir: *Kyrie eleison* (from *Officium Defunctorum*) – Tomás Luis de Victoria (public domain, published by Oxenford Imprint)
Choir: *Emendemus in melius* – Vicente Lusitano (OUP)
Choir: 'Wash me throughly' – Samuel Sebastian Wesley (public domain, published in *Ash Wednesday to Easter*, OUP)

'From ashes to the living font'

- Alan Hommerding is an American writer and composer who was born in 1956. His hymn 'From ashes to the living font' has different verses suitable to be sung on the various Sundays of Lent. Among its themes are the water from the rock in Exodus, the transfiguration, the calling-out of Bartimaeus, and the Samaritan woman at the well. The tune 'Bangor' was written in the eighteenth century by prolific composer William Tans'ur.

Hymn: 'From ashes to the living font' (Bangor)

'Media vita'

- 'Media vita' was commissioned in 2015 to celebrate 500 years since the birth of the English Renaissance composer John Shepherd. The text was used by Thomas Cranmer as part of the funeral service in the Book of Common Prayer: 'In the midst of life we are in death. Whom can we seek as our helper but you, O Lord, who for our sins are justly angry?' John Shepherd, whose 1550s setting of this text is his most highly regarded piece, was master of the choristers at Magdalen College Oxford before joining the choir at the Chapel Royal in London.

Choir: *Media vita* – Kerensa Briggs (OUP)

The Annunciation

Choir: 'Ave Maria' – Robert Parsons (words and music public domain, published in *The Oxford Book of Tudor Anthems*, OUP)

Annunciation

- The annunciation refers to Gabriel's appearance to Mary in Luke 1. It is celebrated on 25 March, known as Lady Day, nine months ahead of Christmas. For a long time, 25 March was marked as the first day of the year. Major celebrations are inhibited by the fact that 25 March almost always falls in Lent: the celebration in Spain was moved to 18 December to avoid this.
- The big theological question is, Was Mary chosen because she was blessed or was she blessed because she was chosen? The Catholic answer tends to be the former, the Protestant one the latter. An old joke tells of how the Protestant went to the pearly gates and met Jesus, who said, 'I don't believe you've met my mother.'

'For Mary, Mother of our Lord'

- John Raphael Peacey (1896–1971) served as a lieutenant in France during World War One, receiving the Military Cross. He played first-class cricket while at Selwyn College, Cambridge. He was headmaster at Bishop Cotton School in Simla, India (1927–35), and then became Principal of Bishop's College, Calcutta (1935–45). He returned to Britain as Canon at Bristol Cathedral.
- Five of his hymns were first published in *100 Hymns for Today* (1969), including 'Filled with the Spirit's power' and this one.

Hymn: 'For Mary, Mother of our Lord' (St Botolph)

Three anthems

- In 1930, when Benjamin Britten was 16 years old, he had a high temperature and was sent to the infirmary at Gresham's School. He read John Buchan novels and revised Chaucer for his exams; and also found time to compose 'A hymn to the Virgin'. The text is by an anonymous poet and dates from around 1300. It appears in *The Oxford Book of English Verse 1250–1900*, which Britten won as a school prize for music. He revised the anthem in 1934 for publication. The main body of the choir sings in Middle English and another group supplies a refrain in Latin. It was first performed in Lowestoft in 1931.

- 'There is no rose' is a carol from the first half of the fifteenth century. It comes from a roll of three pieces of vellum stitched together to form a strip six feet long. It contains 13 carols, including one celebrating Henry V's victory at Agincourt in 1415. The virtue of the rose in the first line is not just goodness and purity, but a special healing power of a plant. One commentator suggests that 'There is no rose of such power' would be a better translation, since virtue originally meant power. Mary is often linked to a rose, as in the carol 'A spotless rose'. This carol sums up Mary's significance in the lines, 'In this rose contained was Heaven and earth in little space.' This setting is by Lucy Walker, composer-in-residence at St Martin-in-the-Fields.
- The Manchester Carols, first performed in 2007, represent a collaboration between the former poet laureate Carol Ann Duffy and the composer Sasha Johnson Manning. Together with a narration, these carols describe the Christmas story in the context of the twenty-first century. The carols work on two levels: first, they highlight the edgy parts of the familiar story, picking out the selflessness of Christ and his concern as an adult for those on whom society turns its back; but second, they remain always alert to the Christian reading of the story: in Athanasius' words, he became what we are that we might become what he is.

Choir: 'A hymn to the Virgin' – Benjamin Britten (Boosey & Hawkes)
Choir: 'There is no rose' – Lucy Walker (OUP)
Choir: 'The Annunciation' (from *Manchester Carols*) – Sasha Johnson Manning (Faber)

'Tell out, my soul'

- This is Timothy Dudley-Smith's first and most famous hymn, written in 1966. The tune was written by Walter Greatorex in 1916. A teacher at Gresham's in Norfolk, Greatorex taught Benjamin Britten, W. H. Auden and Lennox Berkeley. Auden said that Albert Schweitzer played the organ no better than Greatorex.

Hymn: 'Tell out, my soul' (Woodlands)

'Hail Holy Queen'

- The film *Sister Act* tells how nightclub singer Deloris, hidden in a convent as part of a witness protection programme, transforms the desultory convent choir into a rock and roll band. The change is epitomized in its vigorous performance of this song, with conventional words of Marian devotion depicting the Queen of Heaven reigning with seraphim and cherubim.

Choir: 'Hail Holy Queen' (from *Sister Act*) – arr. Roger Emerson/adapt. Marc Shaiman (Hal Leonard)

Holy Week

Choir: 'It is a thing most wonderful' (from St John Passion) – Bob Chilcott (OUP)

Holy Week

- There are two ways to think about the holy days of Maundy Thursday, Good Friday and Easter Day. One is that they are like the three core days of existence – that all existence revolves around them, gaining its meaning in relation to them. In them we find out what love means, what food is for, how precious yet fragile relationships are, how low we can go, how wondrous is God's mercy. They become the touchstone to evaluate all other reality.
- The other way to think about the triduum, as these three days are traditionally known, is to see them as the whole of reality – to perceive everything we do, and everything anyone has ever done, as somehow located within these three days, which comprise the full range of animal, vegetable and mineral experience, embracing, for example, the rooster (that crows), the wine (that's poured) and the stone (that rolls away).

St John Passion

- Bob Chilcott's setting of the Passion is an hour-long work telling the story of Christ's trial and crucifixion following the text from John's Gospel. It was written specially for the Choir of Wells Cathedral for performance on Palm Sunday, 23 March 2013. Within this work Chilcott sets five Passiontide hymn texts ('It is a thing most wonderful', 'Drop, drop, slow tears', 'Jesu, grant me this, I pray', 'There is a green hill far away' and 'When I survey the wondrous cross'), which are designed to be sung by the choir and congregation together. Chilcott himself said, 'It is the austerity, the agony, and ultimately the grace of this story that has inspired me to write this piece, which was performed for the first time in a magnificent building where this same story has been commemorated for almost a thousand years.'

'My song is love unknown'

- This hymn was written by the seventeenth-century Dean of Bristol, Samuel Crossman. His poetry perfectly expresses the essence of God's presence with us in Christ in the line 'Love to the loveless shown that they might lovely be'. Crossman echoes the words of Athanasius, 'He became what we are that we might become what he is.' The hymn highlights the irony that Jesus is hated for healing people, and that the crowd choose a murderer rather than the prince of life.
- In the end, irony, wonder and paradox are all transformed into praise, as Crossman says, 'This is my friend in whose sweet praise I all my days could gladly spend.'
- Crossman clearly knew well the work of George Herbert, because his line 'Never was grief like thine' echoes Herbert's poem 'The Sacrifice'.
- John Ireland wrote the tune 'Love Unknown' specially for this hymn in 1919 and it quickly replaced the original.

Hymn: 'My song is love unknown' (Love unknown)

Three anthems

- Orlando Gibbons was from 1610 to 1625 the leading composer and organist in England. He was a significant figure in the development of the English madrigal. One music critic called him the English Palestrina. He died suddenly aged 41. 'Drop, drop, slow tears' is among his best-loved hymn tunes and Vaughan Williams combined it in the *English Hymnal* with Phineas Fletcher's seventeenth-century text. Phineas Fletcher was a prolific author who flourished during Charles I's reign. Chilcott makes an ambitious move by offering a new setting.
- 'Jesu, grant me this, I pray' is a translation of the original seventeenth-century Latin hymn *'Dignare me, O Jesu, rogo te'*. The translation was made by Henry Williams Baker, who compiled the first edition of *Hymns Ancient & Modern* in 1861. He inherited a baronetcy in 1859. This is another hymn that was previously linked to a tune by Orlando Gibbons.
- The idea for a series of hymns on the Apostles' Creed came from Cecil Frances Alexander's godsons, who complained that the catechism, which they were learning for confirmation, was uninteresting. So she wrote a set of verses illustrating the different clauses of the creed for their benefit. 'There is a green hill far away' refers to 'suffered under Pontius Pilate'.

Choir: 'Drop, drop, slow tears' (from *St John Passion*) – Bob Chilcott (OUP)
Choir: 'Jesu, grant me this, I pray' (from *St John Passion*) – Bob Chilcott (OUP)
Choir: 'There is a green hill far away' (from *St John Passion*) – Bob Chilcott (OUP)

'Were you there when they crucified my Lord?'

- 'Were you there when they crucified my Lord?' is a many-layered spiritual. By drawing attention to presence, it highlights the shortcomings of Jesus' first disciples who weren't present because they had betrayed, denied and fled. By describing events so succinctly yet vividly, the intensity of the action is such that believers feel they actually were there. But by being a spiritual, and thus rooted in the experience of slavery, the song identifies the oppression of its original singers as an experience comparable to that of crucifixion.
- Finally there lies in this song a profound call to ministry and mission. Just as the parable of the sheep and the goats in Matthew 25 points out that when disciples fed the hungry or clothed the stranger they were, without realizing, doing so to Jesus, so this spiritual impels the believer to be there wherever a brother or sister is being crucified by oppression today.

Hymn: 'Were you there when they crucified my Lord?' (Were you there?)

'When I survey the wondrous cross'

- 'When I survey the wondrous cross' is perhaps the best-loved of all passiontide hymns: Matthew Arnold regarded it as the greatest hymn in the English language. It's a constant to-and-fro between the cross and the believer, in the twin mood of love and sorrow, sorrow and love. It's laced with scriptural allusions, such as 'God forbid that I should glory save in the cross of Christ' from Galatians 6. But it's actually an innovation, in that it's among the first hymns to depart from being largely a rendition of specific scriptural texts. The theology is Abelardian: Peter Abelard is associated with a 'subjective' understanding of the atonement, by which what's taking place is not so much the conquering of sin or death as a transformation in the heart of the believer. Accordingly, here the true event that happens on Good Friday is that the believer's heart is moved to devotion and repentance. It begins with 'I survey' and ends with 'my soul, my life, my all'. What Christ's death achieves cosmically is never stated.

Choir: 'When I survey the wondrous cross' (from *St John Passion*) – Bob Chilcott (OUP)

Easter

Choir: 'This joyful Eastertide' – arr. Philip Ledger (Encore Publications or *Ash Wednesday to Easter*, OUP)

Easter

- Easter Day is the central day in the Christian imagination, because it's the single day that contains all the other principal days in the scriptural story. It's a new creation, because in Jesus and Mary it depicts once again a man and a woman in a garden, and it proclaims that all is made new. It's a new exodus, because since the very beginning Christians have identified it as a reprise of the story by which Moses took the Israelites out of slavery to freedom; in this case, the slavery of sin and death is even greater than the slavery of subservience to Pharaoh. It's a new covenant, because it announces that the old covenant with Israel is not invalidated by the sin that led to the exile, but is instead transformed to be for all people. It's a new Christmas, because it's a rebirth of God among us, beyond the clutches of death. It's a reversal of Good Friday, because while on Good Friday we see that nothing can separate God from us, so at Easter we see nothing can separate us from God. And it's a prefigurement of the last day, because everything the last day promises – forgiveness and eternal life – is embodied on Easter Day.
- Easter is awash with metaphors. Many speak of triumph, victory and conquest. For example, the hymn 'Thine be the glory' celebrates the risen conquering son and the endless victory over death. This presents a problem for Christians. Jesus is not a warrior who returns in glory from a successful earthly campaign in which death and sin are defeated. He's the one who shows us the love that will not let us go. That means the way Jesus overcomes death must be consistent with the character of the God who dwells with us for ever. Thus ultimately metaphors of conquest don't do full justice to the Easter story, and it's better to highlight the metaphors that speak of Jesus outlasting death or out-narrating evil. The love that Jesus embodied was something death could not contain: Easter shows us that God's original purpose never to be except to be with us cannot finally be thwarted.

'Now the green blade rises'

- John Macleod Campbell Crum, who was born in 1872, was Rector of Farnham and later a Canon of Canterbury Cathedral. He wrote these words for the tune 'Noël Nouvelet', derived from a fifteenth-century French tune. He was the grandson of the nineteenth-century Scottish theologian John McLeod Campbell, whose notion of universal atonement and the continuity between Christ's ministry and his death were well ahead of his time and have been influential on Scottish theology through Donald Baillie to Thomas Torrance. The hymn begins with John 12.23–24: 'Unless a grain of wheat falls into the earth and dies, it remains just a single grain; but if it dies, it bears much fruit.' It vividly renders Jesus' description of his own resurrection: 'laid in the earth like grain that sleeps unseen'.

Hymn: 'Now the green blade rises' (Noël Nouvelet)

Three anthems

- There are several parts to the Easter Vigil, known as the 'Mother of all vigils': the blessing of the new fire and procession into the church, and the singing of the Exsultet; readings from the Old Testament, including the exodus and the valley of the dry bones, and then the New Testament readings for the Eucharist; the blessing of the font and renewal of baptismal promises; and the Eucharistic liturgy. The Exsultet – named after its first word, 'Exsultet' ('Rejoice!') – originates in the fourth and fifth centuries in the churches of Spain, Italy and France. The text used today was written at some time between the fifth and seventh centuries. After initial sentences exhorting creation and church to praise, it recounts the wonders of the saving work of Christ, whose risen light, shining in the darkness, is represented by the paschal candle. The prayer tells of Christ's work, completed at Easter, prefigured in the Old Testament. This is the night when Christ paid Adam's debt to the eternal Father with his own blood. This is the night of the Passover, when Christ, the true Lamb, was slain to save Israel from slavery. This is the night when Christ, the pillar of fire, led his people through the Red Sea and the desert from slavery to freedom. This is the night when Adam's fault won for the world so great a redeemer, when God gave his own Son to ransom a slave.
- In his compelling 'I know that my redeemer lives', Richard Jeffrey-Grey offers a remarkable Easter anthem in significant contrast to the version in Handel's *Messiah*. Rather than strike a note of triumph, the anthem presents a view of resurrection that is persistent, undaunted and emotionally encompassing. Richard Jeffrey-Grey is Director of Music at Clifton Cathedral in Bristol.
- 'Ye choirs of new Jerusalem' is a medieval hymn written by Fulbert, Bishop of Chartres from 1006 to 1028. It was translated in the 1840s by Robert Campbell, a Scottish Episcopalian who became a lawyer and translated many Latin hymns. He became a Roman Catholic in 1852. The second verse conflates Jesus as Judah's lion from Revelation 5.5 with the notion of crushing the serpent's head from Genesis 3.15. The hymn also draws on the medieval legend of the harrowing of hell.

Choir: 'The Easter Song of Praise' (Exsultet) – Richard Shephard (RSCM)
Choir: 'I know that my redeemer lives' – Richard Jeffrey-Grey (Hoxa Press)
Choir: 'Ye choirs of new Jerusalem' – Charles Villiers Stanford (public domain, published in *Ash Wednesday to Easter*, OUP)

'Alleluia, Alleluia, Hearts to heaven and voices raise'

- This hymn of Bishop Christopher Wordsworth owes its fame to the tune written by Arthur Sullivan, before his celebrated association with W. S. Gilbert. Wordsworth focuses on the notion of Christ as the firstfruits of those who sleep, found in 1 Corinthians 15.20, and goes on to argue, with Paul, that in Christ's resurrection lies our own resurrection – one that will bear much fruit, a reference to John 12.24. Wordsworth was nephew of the poet and became Bishop of Lincoln.

Hymn: 'Alleluia, Alleluia, Hearts to heaven and voices raise' (Lux Eoi)

'Christ the Lord is risen today'

- Charles Wesley included this hymn, with 11 verses, in his 1739 collection, but John Wesley omitted it from his 1780 collection, so it was slow to gain recognition among Methodists. When it was included in the *English Hymnal* in 1906, its first verse was left out, being considered too easily confused with other such hymns, and it became widely known by the first line of its second verse, 'Love's redeeming work'. Eleanor Daley's setting captures its majestic proclamation.

Choir: 'Christ the Lord is risen today' – Eleanor Daley (OUP)

Ascension

Choir: *Coelos ascendit hodie* – Charles Villiers Stanford (public domain, published by Boosey & Hawkes)

Ascension

- Rather like Christmas, it's hard to decide whether the Ascension of our Lord is a glorious celebratory occasion or a quiet, subtle one. The sequence of events followed by the Church is entirely based on the Gospel of Luke and the first chapter of Acts. Unlike John, Luke describes no resurrection appearances beyond Easter Day itself, and its account of the Ascension is mysterious. But the opening chapter of Acts, almost certainly written by the same author, describes Jesus taking the 11 disciples with him to an unknown place, giving them some final instructions, and then ascending until a cloud hid him from their sight. Then two men in white robes foretell that Jesus will return the same way he departed. There's no triumphal departure, but the Church has often chosen to mark the Ascension with tremendous celebration, since it marks the completion of Christ's ministry on earth.
- Ascension tends to be neglected in the Church's imagination. Those who get stuck on the physics of it find it hard to see past ancient paintings where Jesus' feet are glimpsed disappearing out of the top of the picture. Those for whom faith is largely a matter of personal piety concentrate on letting Jesus reign as king of their hearts. But Ascension is centrally about Jesus, having overcome death and been reconciled with his fragile disciples, now taking his place at the right hand of the Father to reign till the last day.

'Hail the day that sees him rise'

- This hymn is an unembarrassed celebration of a triple-decker universe, with earth in between the joys of heaven above and the fires of hell below. Charles Wesley published it in *Hymns and Sacred Poems* in 1739. It is notable that while Christ rejoices on returning to heaven in triumph, we're reminded that 'still he loves the earth he leaves'. Its themes run close to the collect for Ascension Day about how we may in heart and mind continually dwell with the ascended Christ. John Wesley omitted this hymn from an influential 1780 collection because it exalted the liturgical year rather than the experience of the individual disciple. The tune was written by W. H. Monk for the first edition of *Hymns Ancient & Modern* in 1861.

Hymn: 'Hail the day that sees him rise' (Llanfair)

Three anthems

- Psalm 47 is closely associated with the Ascension, and once one appreciates the coyness early composers had about setting the actual words of Jesus, it becomes easier to see how the psalms retained their central place in liturgical worship. Orlando Gibbons' setting 'O clap your hands' and Gerald Finzi's 'God is gone up' are both based on this same psalm. Ascension is the great day that recognizes the different realms of heaven and earth, and should focus the mind on the contrast between what lasts for ever and what does not. But the continued use of Psalm 47 in liturgical treatments does tend to draw attention to the vexed question of whether Jesus physically ascends vertically into the sky.
- George Herbert's hymn 'King of glory, King of peace' is inspired by the psalms of praise, especially Psalm 116. The collect for George Herbert picks up on this hymn, and goes like this: 'King of glory, King of peace, who called your servant George Herbert from the pursuit of worldly honours to be a priest in the temple of his God and King: grant us also the grace to offer ourselves with singleness of heart in humble obedience to your service; through Jesus Christ your Son our Lord.'

Choir: 'O clap your hands' – Orlando Gibbons (public domain, published in *The Oxford Book of Tudor Anthems*, OUP)
Choir: 'King of glory, King of peace' – Grayston Ives (RSCM)
Choir: 'God is gone up' – Gerald Finzi (Boosey & Hawkes)

'Crown him with many crowns'

- Matthew Bridges published this hymn in 1851 and it was included in the Appendix to *Hymns Ancient & Modern* in 1868. It was first written in six verses before six more were added. Jesus is first the lord of love, by suffering for us, then the lord of peace, by inaugurating his kingdom, and finally the lord of time, the alpha and the omega. There is a subtle series of references to Mary. Christ is both her son (fruit of the mystic rose) and her creator (the stem), and also the root of mercy. Some early readers disliked such an intense emphasis on Mary, which they saw as too Catholic.
- The tune 'Diademata' (Greek for crowns) was written by Sir George Elvey, long-time organist of St George's Chapel, Windsor, for *Hymns Ancient & Modern*. It is in keeping with the atmosphere of glory and triumph the hymn evokes.

Hymn: 'Crown him with many crowns' (Diademata)

'Let all the world in every corner sing'

- George Herbert's 'Let all the world in every corner sing' draws out the four places where God is to be worshipped: the heavens, the earth, the Church and, lastly, and for Herbert most importantly, the heart. Herbert was a great student of the human heart and its appropriate affections. The heart must 'bear the longest part' – and continue to praise God even after the worship in church has finished.
- Sally Albrecht was born in Ohio and lives in Raleigh, North Carolina. She has more than 600 popular choral publications in print. Her version takes the first line of Herbert's poem but then improvises her own vision of the universality of God's praise.

Choir: 'Let all the world in every corner sing' – Sally Albrecht (Alfred Publishing Co.)

Pentecost

Choir: 'Come, holy Ghost' – Thomas Attwood (public domain)

Pentecost

- The Holy Spirit often seems to be the poor relation in the Trinity. So much emphasis is placed on Jesus, and God the Father so often resembles the singular God of pre-Trinitarian faith, that the Holy Spirit, as one theologian put it, is always dressed in hand-me-downs. One Reformation debate helps explain the significance of the Holy Spirit. Martin Luther maintained that because Jesus was God, God is everywhere, so it was perfectly possible for Jesus to be present in the bread and wine at holy communion. John Calvin countered that Jesus is fully human so can only be in one place at a time, so is at the right hand of the Father in heaven. The Holy Spirit's work is to make Christ present, so the Holy Spirit makes Christ present in the bread and wine of holy communion. Calvin's way of putting things is immensely helpful, and helps us recognize the Holy Spirit at work in church and world, making Jesus present in friend and stranger.
- Just as Catholics focus their understanding of the Holy Spirit on what takes place in transforming bread and wine into Christ's body and blood, so evangelicals see the Holy Spirit's work primarily in the inspiration of Scripture and the capacity of the preached word to make Christ present in the heart of the believer. Charismatics, meanwhile, tend to associate the Holy Spirit more with the

direct action of God in marvellous events, like healing, prophecy and speaking in tongues. The broad Church has seldom articulated a fully fledged doctrine of the Holy Spirit.

- A real exploration of the work of the Holy Spirit would certainly describe how the Holy Spirit works through the acts of the Church – through the absolving of sins, the preaching of the word, the anointing of the sick, the washing of feet, the baptizing of new believers, and so on. But just as importantly and perhaps more mysteriously, it would make clear how the Holy Spirit works beyond the Church, in the hearts of people far and wide, in the transformation of unjust structures, and in the surprises and discoveries of new life and old truth. For each one of us, it's both wonderful and unsettling to perceive the action of the Holy Spirit in our own lives from their very beginning – indeed never more than in the conception that brought us into existence. The moment when all of these insights come together is in prayer when, as Paul tells us, the Holy Spirit gives us words to say and hears our sighs too deep for words.

'O thou who camest from above'

- This is a classic Charles Wesley hymn taking Leviticus 6.13 ('the fire shall ever be burning upon the altar; it shall never go out') and applying it to the human heart. The hymn was originally two 8-line stanzas, but S. S. Wesley's tune made it four 4-line stanzas. The poetry excels, not least in the remarkable 6-syllable 'inextinguishable'.

Hymn: 'O thou who camest from above' (Hereford)

Three anthems

- George Wither lived from 1588 to 1667. He was a poet, pamphleteer and satirist. He was several times imprisoned. One critic wrote, 'Wither was a man of real genius, but seems to have been partially insane.' In his early twenties he wrote *Abuses Stript and Whipt*, twenty satires directed against Revenge, Ambition, and Lust. The volume included a poem called 'The Scourge', which attacked the Lord Chancellor. This led to Wither being imprisoned for four months. In the 1620s, Wither became a Puritan, as he started to embrace the Calvinist doctrine of predestination. In 1623 he published *Hymns and Songs of the Church*, and obtained from King James I an ordinance that it should be bound up with every copy of the authorized metrical psalms offered for sale. This ordinance was annulled a couple of years later, and Wither published a diatribe against those he held responsible for his ruin. In the Civil War Wither fought for Parliament; but he fell out with Cromwell. He was imprisoned for three years at the Restoration,

and by his death had become a Quaker. His life is almost the opposite of the peaceful image of George Herbert and is like a parable of the turbulent times of the seventeenth century. This Pentecost anthem by Orlando Gibbons appears in Wither's 1623 hymn book.
- Ralph Vaughan Williams was born in 1872. Three key periods in his life were his collecting folksongs around 1900, fighting in World War One in his forties, and his late-life 1930s love affair with Ursula, who became his second wife in the 1950s. With Percy Dearmer he spent two years compiling the *English Hymnal*, published in 1906. The first edition was censured by the Archbishop of Canterbury. It was much influenced by Robert Bridges' *Yattendon Hymnal* a decade before and it was triggered by failure of the 1904 revision of *Hymns Ancient & Modern*. 'Come down O love divine' was typical: it was a fourteenth-century Italian hymn, translated in 1861. Vaughan Williams composed the tune and named it after the village of his birth in Gloucestershire. It was sung at his funeral in Westminster Abbey in 1958 as his ashes were interred in Musicians' Corner.
- Alison Willis is a contemporary composer who works with all things historical, particularly medieval sources and forgotten texts written by women. 'Like the dove' was published in 2018. It is a simple setting of a text from the Anglo-Saxon 'Old English Martyrology' for Pentecost: 'The Spirit dwells in all those who do good, and it rejoices in the heart of a true man, like the Dove when she bathes in quiet waters.'

Choir: 'Come, Holy Ghost, the maker come' – Orlando Gibbons (public domain)
Choir: 'Come down, O love divine' – William Harris (Novello)
Choir: 'Like the dove' – Alison Willis (Encore Publications)

'Come, Holy Spirit, come'

- Michael Forster was provoked into writing this hymn after hearing a speaker describe the gifts of the Holy Spirit with regard to their edification for worshippers, without a sense of how they could be a gift for others. It was written for this tune, associated with 'Crown him with many crowns'. Forster was first a Baptist and then a United Reformed Church minister, having begun as a music teacher. He has written 600 hymns and several Christian musicals.

Hymn: 'Come, Holy Spirit, come' (Diademata)

'Ev'ry time I feel the Spirit'

- This glorious spiritual keeps the narrative structure of Covenant – Baptism – Heaven, broadly matching the sequence of Old Testament events. It thus embodies the proximity that spirituals tend to keep with key Old Testament events together with an emphasis on heavenly glory. William Dawson captures the joy of the Spirit in this exuberant celebration.

Choir: 'Ev'ry time I feel the Spirit' – Spiritual arr. William Dawson (OUP)

Harvest

Choir: 'Look at the world' – John Rutter (OUP)

Harvest

- The tradition of a harvest festival in the form we know it today, with produce, sometimes a supper, decorations, processions and often a shapely loaf, began in 1843 at Morwenstow, the most northerly parish in Cornwall. The vicar, Robert Hawker, was an eccentric: he was renowned for dressing up as a mermaid and excommunicating his cat for mousing on Sundays. His first wife was 22 years older than him; his second wife was 40 years younger than him. At the first harvest festival on 1 October 1843, bread made from the first cut of corn was received at communion.
- Harvest today brings together several themes. Because it often coincides with the feast of St Francis on 4 October, it has become associated with creation care – and in the last few decades that has meant a direct link to the climate emergency. But because of the tradition of bringing produce to be distributed among those with fewer resources, harvest has come to be a time for reflection on issues of just distribution and inequality, global and local. So what started as a simple act of thanksgiving is now a profound examination of a network of dependencies, on God, one another and the planet.
- The theological heart of harvest is as the place where the beginning of God's story meets the end. It's a celebration of creation, in hymns like 'Fair waved the golden corn' and 'Come, ye thankful people, come'; but it's also an anticipation of the last day, with its harvest images of reaping and threshing.

Harvest

'Come, ye thankful people, come'

- Henry Alford was a Victorian theologian and artist and, from 1857 until his death in 1871, Dean of Canterbury. He had spent 18 years as Rector of Wymeswold in Leicestershire, and had a good sense of the rural traditions that the new practice of harvest festivals brought within the church building. He sprinkles his hymn with Jesus' agrarian stories – of wheat and tares, and of the sower. The energetic tune was written by Sir George Elvey, long time organist at St George's Chapel, Windsor, and is named accordingly.

Hymn: 'Come, ye thankful people, come' (St George's Windsor)

Three anthems

- The hymn 'To thee, O Lord, our hearts we raise' was written by William Chatterton Dix (1837–98), who also wrote 'As with gladness men of old' and 'Alleluia! Sing to Jesus', just a year after the Church of England had first published an order of service for harvest festival. The hymn begins with harvest references from Psalm 65.9–13, but then moves in verse 2 to the bread of life discourse in John 6.32–58, and a vision of the last judgement as harvest. Then in verse 3 there is a reference to Psalm 126.6: 'he shall come again with joy, bringing his sheaves with him', which is return from exile. Then the climax is from Revelation 4.6–11, a further journey to Zion. June Nixon (born 1942) is an Australian organist and composer. Here in her 2005 anthem she provides an alternative setting to the familiar Arthur Sullivan tune.
- Maurice Greene (1695–1755) was a choirboy at St Paul's and later became the organist there, as well as at the Chapel Royal. In 1730 he became Professor of Music at Cambridge University. In 1735 he was appointed Master of the King's Musick. In this anthem, with words taken from Psalm 65, he reflects on God's threefold action of visiting the earth, blessing it and crowning it: here there is a subtle reference to the Christological manner of Jesus' visiting, blessing and crowning creation, just as the Holy Spirit does the same in bringing fruit from the soil.
- The Benedicite consists of verses 35–65 of the Song of the Three Children, an apocryphal addition to Daniel 3. It is Shadrach, Meschach and Abednego's hymn of praise on deliverance from the fiery furnace into which they had been thrown by Nebuchadnezzar. Francis Jackson was a longtime director of music at York Minster; he died in 2022.

Choir: 'Harvest carol' – June Nixon (Encore Publications)
Choir: 'Thou visitest the earth' – Maurice Greene (public domain)
Choir: Benedicite in G – Francis Jackson (Banks Music Publications)

'For the fruits of all creation'

- This is a classic Fred Pratt Green hymn – direct, useful, easy to sing and laden with simple theological themes – and the occasion of rediscovery of a neglected tune. He wrote it in 1970. It anticipates the contemporary sense of harvest: reward for work, care for the hungry, and just distribution of the fruits of the earth. In a subtle reference to Deuteronomy 24, Green points out the Old Testament tradition that once the harvest is done, the corners of the field are for the stranger, the orphan and the widow. The tune by Francis Jackson had been written for 'God that madest earth and heaven' but had been displaced by the 'All through the night' setting. So it was ripe for reassignment.

Hymn: 'For the fruits of all creation' (East Acklam)

'All good gifts' (from *Godspell*)

- This is an abbreviated version of 'We plough the fields and scatter', which was written by Matthias Claudius (1740–1815) from Lübeck in Schleswig-Holstein. Claudius is chiefly known for writing 'Death and the Maiden', which became famous after Schubert made an arrangement of it for his String Quartet No. 14 in D minor.
- This version was written for the final incarnation of *Godspell* at the Cherry Lane Theatre in Greenwich Village, New York. Schwartz was inspired, in part, by the introductory chords to James Taylor's song 'Fire and Rain'.

Choir: 'All good gifts' (from *Godspell*) – Stephen Schwartz arr. John LeAvitt (Hal Leonard)

All Saints

Choir: *O quam gloriosum* – Tomás Luis de Victoria (public domain)

All Saints

- All Saints is a rather confusing date in the Church's calendar. That's because the Church tends to give out conflicting messages about what All Saints means. In some circles All Saints is a way of talking about the communion between the living and the dead. It's a way of celebrating that when we're in Christ we can be united with those believers who have gone before us in the faith. In other circles All Saints is a kind of Oscar ceremony, where we hand out prizes to those who have been outstanding examples in the faith, and we recall stories of those who have been tortured and martyred and in a myriad of other ways have qualified to be put in a stained glass window. This makes All Saints a kind of spectator sport, which has nothing much to do with us. So in modern times there has been what we might call a democratic reaction to such elitism, and an insistence that we all get to be saints. But this leaves us with a sneaking anxiety that we've been given the candy without eating the savoury course first, so All Saints finally ends up becoming a pep rally where we hit each other's chests and pump iron and tell each other to be more muscular Christians than we were an hour ago.

'For all thy saints, O Lord'

- Richard Mant was a chaplain to the Archbishop of Canterbury before becoming a bishop in the Church of Ireland from 1820 to 1848. He was most celebrated as a translator of hymns from the Latin. He also wrote his own hymns, including 'Bright the vision that delighted' and this one for All Saints. The tune 'Mount Ephraim' was composed by Benjamin Milgrove, a fancy goods retailer in Bath in the 1700s.

Hymn: 'For all thy saints, O Lord' (Mount Ephraim)

Three anthems

- 'Hark! I hear the harps eternal' is a classic American revival song that pictures the glorious welcome that awaits the justified sinner on entering the heavenly realms. Harps were particularly fashionable in nineteenth-century Appalachia, where this song originated. Alice Parker was an American composer from Boston, Massachusetts who died in 2023.
- Isaac Watts took this description of the veil that shields heaven from our earthly eyes, and turned it into a fervent prayer that we might be given the wings of faith to rise within that veil and see the life of the saints who once dwelt as we do with sins and doubts and fears but now are surrounded by joys and glories. He then turns from intercession to imagination, as he depicts himself asking the blessed ones whence cometh their victory – and the saints with one accord attribute it to Christ's sacrifice as the Lamb of God. Finally, he turns again, this time to preach and call on the singer to follow in Christ's footsteps. What's fascinating about this hymn is that Watts makes the ingredients of his parents' Puritan faith – tribulation, walking with Christ, zeal and victory – the constituents of a universal gospel.

- In 'Christus est stella', Will Todd sets words by the Venerable Bede, from his commentary on Revelation 2.28, which are also found inscribed above Bede's tomb in the Galilee Chapel of Durham Cathedral. Todd's anthem interweaves the original Latin text with an English translation, in a work that is both ecstatic and contemplative. The words are from 'Christ in glory': Christ is the Morning Star, who when the night of this world is past, gives to his saints the promise of the light of life, and opens everlasting day.

Choir: 'Hark! I hear the harps eternal' – trad. hymn arr. Alice Parker (Lawson-Gould)
Choir: 'Give us the wings of faith' – James Whitbourn (Chester Music)
Choir: *Christus est stella* – Will Todd (OUP)

'For all the saints'

- William Walsham How began to write hymns for services he shared as a child with his siblings. He became a Tractarian while at Oxford in the 1840s and remained an advocate of the Oxford Movement throughout his ministry. He was for 28 years Rector of Whittington in Shropshire, where he wrote this hymn, before becoming the 'omnibus bishop', working in the East End of London and taking only public transport. He later became the first Bishop of Wakefield. Ralph Vaughan Williams composed the tune for the 1906 *English Hymnal*.

Hymn: 'For all the saints' (Sine Nomine)

'When the saints go marching in'

- This song has no clear origin, but has long been associated with jazz and the city of New Orleans. It echoes many spirituals in looking forward to the inauguration of God's kingdom on the last day – by the use of the term 'number', it suggests the last day is like God's best song.

Choir: 'When the saints go marching in' – arr. John Rutter (OUP)

All Souls

Choir: *Komm, süßer Tod* – Ethyl Smyth (Multitude of Voyces)

All Souls

- All Souls, properly known as the Commemoration of the Faithful Departed, logically belongs in the season of Easter. It was shifted to November in 998 by Odilo, Abbot of Cluny. The Orthodox still mark the date during the Easter season.
- Its theological basis is as an occasion for prayer for those in purgatory. In the Apocrypha, 2 Maccabees 12 affirms the efficacy of prayers for the dead. The practice goes back to the earliest days of Christians in the catacombs, and is mentioned by Tertullian. But it's been a flashpoint since the Reformation, as Protestants have often objected that purgatory and prayers for the departed have no place in a religion of justification by grace through faith.

'My soul, there is a country'

- Henry Vaughan was born in Breconshire in 1622 into an impoverished family. He was educated by a clergyman-schoolmaster and then attended Jesus College, Oxford, long regarded as the Welsh college. He left two years later without completing his degree and studied law in London. He fought for the Royalists in the Civil War. He died in 1695.
- This is a meditation on the 'peace of God, which passes all understanding' – a phrase from Philippians 4 made familiar by its frequent use in the blessing at the end of the Eucharist. Henry Vaughan offers a five-sentence prayer, addressing his soul. He imagines heaven, where peace reigns, where an angel knows what terrible things take place on earth. In heaven, command lies with one born in a manger who is our gracious friend. The poem finishes intriguingly with the line 'Thy God, thy life, thy cure', made more significant by the fact that Vaughan practised medicine in his Welsh village of Llansantffraed, Powys.

Hymn: 'My soul, there is a country' (Christus der ist mein leben)

Three anthems

- Absalom was the third son of David, and the most handsome man in the kingdom; but he rebelled against his father. He murdered his elder brother Amnon for assaulting his sister Tamar. He spent four years preparing to attack

David, before the eventual battle at Ephraim's Wood. His army was routed, and Absalom's head was caught in the boughs of an oak tree as the mule he was riding ran beneath it. David's commander Joab thereupon killed him. David's lament echoes through the Bible: 'O my son Absalom, my son, my son Absalom! Would that I had died instead of you, O Absalom, my son, my son!' Its significance is expanded by Jesus' dialogue with his Father from the cross. Thomas Tomkins was born in Pembrokeshire in 1572. He moved to Gloucester by 1594. He became organist at Worcester Cathedral, where he married his predecessor's widow. He composed most of the music for the coronation of Charles I. 'When David heard' was probably composed as a lament for Henry, the young Prince of Wales who died in 1612, and was later published by the composer in a set of madrigals, though it was still sung in religious services. Composed in two sections, the anthem's power lies in its unexpected shift from third-person description to a first-person outpouring of grief – a move that is suddenly and shockingly intimate.

- *Funeral Ikos* was written in 1981 when John Tavener was 37. It is a serene setting of the reward in Paradise for the Righteous Ones. The music shows the influence of Stravinsky. Much of it is in unison, allowing the full impact of the words to shine through.
- Ruth's speech to Naomi in the first chapter of the book of Ruth covers some of the most moving words in the Bible, as Ruth cleaves to her mother-in-law after her husband and brother-in-law have both died. They are words that sum up the power of being with, and a love that transcends death. This setting is by Allan Friedman, former Duke University Chapel Assistant Director of Music.

Choir: 'When David heard' – Thomas Tomkins (public domain, published in *The Oxford Book of Tudor Anthems*, OUP)
Choir: *Funeral Ikos* – John Tavener (Chester Music)
Choir: 'Where'er you go' – Allan Friedman (www.teachingallan.com)

'Soul of my Saviour'

- This is a translation of a Latin hymn dating back at least to the fourteenth century. The hymn conflates the Eucharist, the death of Christ on the cross, and the believer's sanctification in a characteristically Roman Catholic way: the lines 'Blood of my Saviour, bathe me in thy tide' and 'Deep in thy wounds, Lord, hide and shelter me' have a distinctive flavour of nineteenth-century Catholic piety. Its appeal as a funeral hymn and one used with the dying is perceptible from the final verse: 'Lead me from night to never ending day.'

Hymn: 'Soul of my Saviour' (Anima Christi)

'It is well with my soul'

- In 1873, Chicago lawyer Horatio Spafford sent his wife and four daughters to England for a holiday and went to New York to wave them off. Nine days later he received a telegram from his wife with the unimaginably horrifying words, 'Saved alone.' He got the next boat to England, and when the ship passed the point of the tragedy that had claimed his four daughters and 222 others, he went to his cabin and wrote this extraordinary hymn.
- This version was arranged by René Clausen for the Duke University Chapel Choir in 2012.

Choir: 'It is well with my soul' – arr. René Clausen (MorningStar Music Publishers)

Remembrance

Choir: 'Present yourselves as a living sacrifice' – James O'Donnell (Shorter House)

Remembrance Day

- This is a memorial day observed in Commonwealth member states since the end of World War One to honour armed forces members who have died in the line of duty. Following a tradition inaugurated by King George V in 1919, Remembrance Day is observed on 11 November to recall the end of World War One hostilities.
- Hostilities formally ended 'at the 11th hour of the 11th day of the 11th month' of 1918, in accordance with the armistice signed by representatives of Germany and the Entente between 5:12 and 5:20 that morning. World War One officially ended with the signing of the Treaty of Versailles on 28 June 1919.

'O God, our help in ages past'

- Isaac Watts based this hymn on Psalm 90, contrasting the frailty of the human condition with the majesty of God. Its most evocative line is 'Time like an ever-rolling stream …' which speaks to the ephemeral character of human life in a way that links this hymn with the themes of Remembrance.
- The hymn was originally part of *The Psalms of David Imitated in the Language of the New Testament*, published by Watts in 1719. In this book he paraphrased in Christian verse the entire psalter except for 12 psalms which he felt were unsuited for Christian usage.

- The hymn tune 'St Anne' was composed by William Croft in 1708 while he was the organist of the church of St Anne, Soho. He was later organist at Westminster Abbey.

Hymn: 'O God, our help in ages past' (St Anne)

Three anthems

- Born near Altrincham, John Ireland went to the Royal College of Music where he studied under C. V. Stanford. He wrote this anthem in 1912 when he was organist at St Luke's, Chelsea. The anthem engages the question posed by Song of Songs 8: is love stronger than death? It is the question that sums up the whole Bible. Ireland's music says 'Yes', and demonstrates the theology and ethics of yes, including its far-reaching social dimensions. The mood often changes in this anthem. It opens with a broad melody before the tempo heightens to a climax at which point the music settles into a soprano solo – 'Who, his own Self'. A baritone then picks up the theme and the anthem moves into a dramatic fanfare passage before reaching its thrilling climax. The final section sustains the tension which is only relaxed at the very end.
- Eleanor Daley was born in Ontario and has lived most of her life in Toronto. Her a capella requiem mixes Latin and Russian texts with Scripture and more contemporary popular piety. 'In Remembrance' is based on some famous words of Mary Frye. Mary Elizabeth Clark was born in 1905 and was orphaned at the age of 3. In 1927 she married Claud Frye. She wrote her famous poem 'Do not stand at my grave and weep' five years later in 1932. She spent most of her life in Baltimore, MD and died in 2004.
- William Denis Browne was a friend of Rupert Brooke at Rugby and Cambridge. He met many musicians at Cambridge including Vaughan Williams and was regarded as the most promising of them all. He followed a musical career only because his poor result in his finals blocked his path into the civil service. Browne died at Gallipoli in 1915 aged 26. He asked friends to destroy the compositions that weren't his best so fewer than 20 remain, including his Nunc dimittis in A. The Nunc dimittis has profound resonances of farewell and beginning, and is in the context of Simeon telling Mary 'a sword will pierce your own heart also' – a definitive case of a mother getting bad news.

Choir: 'Greater love hath no man' – John Ireland (Stainer & Bell)
Choir: 'In Remembrance' (from Requiem) – Eleanor Daley (Jubilate Music Group)
Choir: Nunc dimittis in A – William Denis Browne (Church Music Society)

'By gracious powers, so wonderfully sheltered'

- Dietrich Bonhoeffer helped to found the Confessing Church in Germany, which opposed the German Christians and stood against Nazism. He formed his own seminary to train clergy of the Confessing Church. In 1939 he had the opportunity to stay in the USA but opted to return to Germany. He was implicated in the plot to kill Hitler and spent the rest of the war in prison. He turned down the chance to escape because doing so would have implicated others. His *Letters and Papers from Prison*, from which this poem comes, were very influential on the post-war reappraisal of theology, including famous phrases like 'religionless Christianity' and 'a world come of age'.

Hymn: 'By gracious powers, so wonderfully sheltered' (Highwood)

'We will remember them (For the fallen)'

- On 23 August 1914, in Britain's opening action of World War One on the Western Front, the British Expeditionary Force was defeated at the Battle of Mons. 'For the Fallen' was specifically composed by Laurence Binyon (1869–1943) in honour of the casualties of the British Expeditionary Force. Binyon composed the original poem while sitting on the cliffs between Pentire Point and the Rumps in north Cornwall.
- It was first published in *The Times* in September 1914. Its tone is much more in keeping with the later stages of war than the gung-ho sentiments of September 1914. Binyon's biographer said, 'By 1918 it was an infinitely better poem than it had been in 1914.'
- The fourth stanza was written first and is today taken alone as a liturgy of remembrance. (People often get the sequence of the words wrong.) The line 'Age shall not weary them' echoes Enobarbus' description of Cleopatra in *Antony and Cleopatra*: 'Age cannot wither her, nor custom stale Her infinite variety.' The line 'Lest we forget', taken from Rudyard Kipling's poem 'Recessional' (which incidentally has nothing to do with remembering the fallen in war), is often added as if it were part of the ode.
- The words are read by a British soldier at the Menin Gate in Ypres every evening at 8pm, after the first part of the Last Post, and followed by a minute of silence.

Choir: 'We will remember them (For the fallen)' – Edward Elgar arr. Ian Tracey (Novello)

HYMNWRITERS

George Herbert

Choir: 'A grateful heart' – Mary Plumstead (Roberton Publications)

George Herbert (1593–1633)

- Born in Wales in 1593 into the aristocratic Pembroke family, George Herbert became Public Orator at Cambridge University and then a Member of Parliament, apparently destined for a life at court. To widespread surprise, he decided to be ordained and, after spending a period with his friend Nicholas Ferrar at Little Gidding, he became incumbent of the parish of Bemerton, near Salisbury.
- There were never more than 100 people in his church. He died after only three years in his parish. He wrote prolifically, his hymns still being popular throughout the English-speaking world. His treatise on the priestly life, *The Country Parson*, and his poetry, especially *The Temple*, earned him a leading place in English literature. He died at the age of 40 in 1633.

'Teach me, my God and King'

- The text for this hymn is from Herbert's poem 'The Elixir'. The hymn talks about finding the divine in the everyday.
- The term the 'philosopher's stone' refers to the ancient practice of alchemy, which sought to turn base metal into gold. The term was made famous by its use in the title of the first *Harry Potter* book. Herbert says the phrase 'for thy sake' turns the humblest action into worship.
- The West Country tune 'Sandys' was first published in William Sandys' *Christmas Carols*, 1833.

Hymn: 'Teach me, my God and King' (Sandys)

George Herbert

Three anthems

- Herbert reflected ruefully on the ambitions he pursued before his call to ordination. 'I can now behold the [King's] Court with an impartial eye, and see plainly that it is made up of fraud, titles and flattery, and many other such empty, imaginary and painted pleasures: pleasures that are so empty as not to satisfy when they are enjoyed.' None of George Herbert's poems were published in his lifetime, but he bequeathed his poems to his friend Nicholas Ferrar, and within 40 years they had gone through 13 editions – a total of more than 20,000 copies – a startling publication run in the mid-seventeenth century.
- Herbert's poem 'Come my way', known as 'The Call', is almost entirely made up of words of one syllable. It's based around Jesus' single-syllable words in John 14, often read at funerals, 'I am the way, the truth, and the life.' Herbert dwells on each term, and adds two other trinities of his own – the light, the feast, and the strength, and the joy, the love and the heart. Richard Lloyd, who died in 2021, was a prolific composer, many of whose 600 compositions were written during his spell as organist of Durham Cathedral in the 1970s.
- George Herbert's hymn 'King of glory, King of peace' is inspired by the psalms of praise, especially Psalm 116. Sir Henry Walford Davies succeeded Edward Elgar as Master of the King's Music, a post he held from 1934 until 1941. He became famous for his BBC broadcasts in the 1920s. His work 'Solemn Melody' has been played at the Cenotaph on Remembrance Sunday since 1930.
- In his poem 'Whitsunday', an excerpt from which forms the anthem 'Listen, sweet dove', Herbert is grieved that the contemporary Church lacks any trace of the apostles' fervour. He longs for a second Pentecost, since it seems the Holy Spirit has not galvanized believers as Christ intended. Grayston Ives is a British composer and was a longstanding organist at Magdalen College, Oxford.

Choir: 'The Call' – Richard Lloyd (RSCM)
Choir: 'King of glory, King of peace' – Henry Walford Davies (Novello)
Choir: 'Listen, sweet dove' – Grayston Ives (RSCM)

'The God of love my shepherd is'

- 'The God of love my shepherd is', based on Psalm 23, is the only psalm in Herbert's collection *The Temple*. While the psalm speaks of kindness, goodness, care and mercy, it never actually mentions the word 'love' – which is an addition of Herbert's, picked up in H. W. Baker's nineteenth-century hymn 'The King of love my shepherd is'. Herbert stresses the relationship between the believer and God, memorably in the words 'He is mine and I am his.'

Hymn: 'The God of love my shepherd is' (University)

'Let all the world'

- When Herbert, on his deathbed at age 39, gave *The Temple* to a friend to take to Nicholas Ferrar, he gave it this inscription: 'Tell him, he shall find in it a picture of the many spiritual Conflicts that have past betwixt God and my Soul, before I could subject mine to the will of Jesus my Master: in whose service I have now found perfect freedom; desire him to read it: and then, if he can think it may turn to the advantage of any dejected poor Soul, let it be made publick: if not, let him burn it: for I and it, are less than the least of God's mercies.'
- Herbert explores four contexts in which God may be praised. He begins with heaven, the throne of grace; he then turns to earth, the scene of Christ's incarnation; he proceeds to the Church, where God's name is recognized and celebrated; and he concludes with the human heart, the seat of sincerity and truth.

Choir: 'Let all the world' – Ralph Vaughan Williams (Stainer & Bell)

John Donne

Choir: 'Prayer of John Donne' – William Bradley Roberts (St James Music Press)

John Donne (1572–1631)

- Donne was a Catholic, and because of this never gained a degree despite attending Oxford University at the age of 11. There were three seasons to his life.
- The first (1572–1601) we can call secular and sensual. He studied to be a lawyer, and in 1592 was admitted to Lincoln's Inn. He began to question his Catholicism after his brother died of the bubonic plague in prison for harbouring a Catholic priest. Donne went on to spend his inheritance on women, literature and travel, and fought briefly against the Spanish, before later being appointed Chief Secretary to the Lord Keeper of the Great Seal at York House on the Strand.
- The second (1601–15) was a period of impoverishment. He married his patron's niece, and was thrown into Fleet prison for this misdemeanour. In his inimitable words, 'John Donne. Anne Donne. Undone.'
- The third (1615–31) was more agreeable. He was ordained, and became Dean of St Paul's Cathedral in 1621. In 1624, after a near-fatal illness, he became Vicar of St Dunstan-in-the-West. He is buried in St Paul's Cathedral.

'Wilt thou forgive that sin, by man begun'

- John Donne's only published hymn was written during his serious illness in the winter of 1623 and entitled 'A Hymne to God the Father'. Donne had this poem set to music and sung at evening service at St Paul's Cathedral. Like Augustine's famous line, 'Make me chaste but not yet', these words show Donne's wrestling with sin and faith in Christ's power to heal beyond death.

Hymn: 'Wilt thou forgive that sin, by man begun' (Dresden)

Three anthems

- In his beautiful prayer, 'Bring us, O Lord God', often read at funerals, Donne speaks of four ways of blending the rest and activity of heaven – light, music, possession, eternity. Some say this poem was a plea for equality in the world to come as Donne was discriminated against for much of his life. The phrase 'one equal music' speaks to the capacity of music to reach everyone, yet in different ways.
- In 'A Hymne to Christ', Donne proclaims that you cannot find the true love of Christ until you love him more than you love anyone in the world. Donne wanted the true love of a woman, but now in 'A Hymne to Christ' he has altered his thinking. Now, he does not want the loyalty of any woman, but loyalty in his love towards Christ. He works with a fundamental image of crossing from sin and death to righteousness and eternal life, with constant imagery of the sea. Imogen Holst, who died in 1984, was the only child of the composer Gustav Holst. For 20 years she was joint artistic director of the Aldeburgh Festival. Much of her music is unpublished and unperformed.
- In 'At the round earth's imagined corners', Donne asks God to teach him how to repent so he can be among the blessed on Judgement Day. Hubert Parry was President of the Music in Wartime committee, which provided opportunities for professional musicians to contribute to the war effort by giving concerts in hospitals and camps. He was a Germanophile and the outbreak of war in 1914 was personally devastating for him. He wrote *Songs of Farewell* in 1916–18, towards the end of his life. The sense of his own death as well as the many deaths of his students and friends is evident. He died of Spanish flu in 1918. The first performance of the complete set of six songs was at a memorial service to Parry held in the chapel of Exeter College, Oxford in February 1919, four months after his death.

Choir: 'Bring us, O Lord God' – William Harris (Novello)
Choir: 'A Hymne to Christ' – Imogen Holst (Boosey & Hawkes)
Choir: 'At the round earth's imagined corners' (from *Songs of Farewell*) – C. H. H. Parry (public domain, published by Cramer Music)

'The God of love my shepherd is'

- This hymn comes from a contemporary of Donne and fellow metaphysical poet, George Herbert. It is from his celebrated posthumous collection *The Temple* and, being a translation of Psalm 23, is the only version of a psalm in the book. There is no mention of love in the original psalm. A constant pattern in the hymn is where Herbert conjoins two divergent things with the same verb. Everything depends on the relationship between the disciple and God: 'while he is mine and I am his …'

Hymn: 'The God of love my shepherd is' (University)

'Sweet stay a while'

- This anthem explores many themes of love – the desire to keep love free from the cares of work and business, but the recognition that if light fell upon all the lovers' activities, it might introduce distrust. Dowland (1563–1626) was principally a lute player, and in 1612 became one of the King's Lutes at a salary of 20 pence a day.

Choir: 'Sweet stay a while' – John Dowland (public domain)

Richard Crashaw

Choir: 'I am all fair' – Andrew Carter (OUP)

Richard Crashaw (1613–49)

- Crashaw was a seventeenth-century metaphysical poet. Born the son of a Puritan minister, he became a fellow at Peterhouse, Cambridge, and an advocate of the high church reforms of Archbishop Laud. He became curate at Little St Mary's. He was much influenced by the community at Little Gidding and its leader Nicholas Ferrar. During the English Civil War he was forced out of Cambridge and went into exile in Rome, where he converted to Roman Catholicism and was employed by Cardinal Pallotta. After being appointed to a canonry at Loreto on the east coast of Italy, he died suddenly four months later at 37, possibly through poisoning.

- His poetry connects the beauty of nature with the spiritual significance of existence, and dwells on the secret architecture of things. Some of his finest work draws on Teresa of Avila, whose writings were not available in English at the time.

'Lord, when the sense of thy sweet grace'

- This is a hymn from Crashaw's poem about the reconciliation of life and death through union with God. It consistently juxtaposes opposites: life in death, joy in pain, love in anguish. Thus, 'I die in love's delicious Fire, and Still live in me this loving strife Of living Death and dying Life,' and also, 'While thou sweetly slayest me.' The original poem was entitled 'Song', so making it a hymn is highly appropriate. It goes to a sixteenth-century German tune.

Hymn: 'Lord, when the sense of thy sweet grace' (Ach bleib bei uns)

Three anthems

- 'Look up, sweet babe' is a setting by Lennox Berkeley of part of Crashaw's 'Hymn for the Epiphany'. The hymn portrays the Christ child as the new light source in the east to replace the sun. Later in the poem Christ's crucifixion is described as the moment when humankind is freed of its idols. One aspect that has drawn much attention is a hint at the *via negativa* – the notion that God can only be described in terms of what God is not – and the way prayer directs the believer not to the sun or the self but to Christ. Sir Lennox Berkeley was a longtime Professor of Composition at the Royal College of Music and close associate of Benjamin Britten. He died in 1989.
- Perhaps Crashaw's best-known words are the opening of this poem, set by the contemporary composer Jonathan Dove: 'Wellcome, all WONDERS in one sight! Æternity shutt in a span. Sommer in Winter. Day in Night. Heaven in earth, & GOD in MAN.' This is Crashaw's rendering of the glorious exchange, by which, as Athanasius put it, he became what we are that we might become what he is. Summer in winter contrasts the ultimate flowering of God's relationship with humanity, and thus the apogee of the year (summer), with the fact that Christmas, when that nativity is celebrated, falls at the coldest time of year (winter). It also contrasts the fullness of human possibility (Jesus) with the true horror of human failure (putting Jesus to death).
- In 1263, a German priest, Peter of Prague, made a pilgrimage to Rome. He stopped in Bolsena, Italy, to celebrate Mass at the church of St Christina. When he recited the prayer of consecration as he celebrated the Mass, blood began to emerge from the consecrated host onto the altar and corporal. Peter reported

this miracle to Pope Urban IV, who was nearby in Orvieto. The Pope ordered the host and corporal be brought to Orvieto. The relics were then placed in the Orvieto Cathedral, where they remain today. This Eucharistic miracle confirmed the visions given to St Juliana of Mont Cornillon in Belgium (1193–1258). Juliana was a nun and mystic who was instructed to establish a liturgical feast for the Holy Eucharist, to which she had a great devotion. Soon after her death, Pope Urban instituted Corpus Christi for the Universal Church and celebrated it for the first time in Orvieto in 1264, a year after the Eucharistic miracle in Bolsena. Gerald Finzi assembled the text from two Crashaw poems, '*Adoro Te*' and '*Lauda Sion Salvatorem*', themselves translations of hymns by Thomas Aquinas.

Choir: 'Look up, sweet babe' – Lennox Berkeley (Chester Music)
Choir: 'Wellcome, all wonders in one sight!' – Jonathan Dove (Faber)
Choir: 'Lo! The full-final sacrifice' – Gerald Finzi (Boosey & Hawkes)

'With all the powers my poor heart hath'

- This is another translation by Crashaw of a hymn by Thomas Aquinas. The hymn is a statement of true worship – bringing all one's powers to humility and loyalty, to lower oneself before the one who lowered himself for us. It reflects on the experience of the Eucharist, in which the bread of life becomes one's own breath, and we may drink the 'unsealed source' of Christ. All of which, proclaims the final verse, is an anticipation of the constant worship of heaven.

Hymn: 'With all the powers my poor heart hath' (Rockingham)

'Summer in winter'

- This is an excerpt from Crashaw's poem 'A Hymn of the Nativity' of which 'Welcome all wonders' forms the third verse. The shepherds, returning from the stable, sing to awaken the sun and announce that tonight they saw something much brighter than he; and they saw by night something much finer than they had ever seen by day. Sasha Johnson Manning is a contemporary composer based in Manchester.

Choir: 'Summer in winter' – Sasha Johnson Manning (Encore Publications)

Isaac Watts

Choir: 'Joy to the world' – arr. Rutter (OUP)

Isaac Watts (1674–1748)

- We take hymns for granted, but they're a constantly evolving form of worship. A hymn is a devotional lyric poem, simple and metrical in form, genuinely emotional, designed to be sung, its ideas so direct and so immediately apparent as to unify a congregation while singing it. Hymns in the vernacular emerged after the Reformation. While Calvin believed in singing only what was directly authorized by the Bible, Luther wrote chorales to teach the faith.
- The key English-speaking figure was Isaac Watts, who died in 1748. Watts didn't just sing psalms – he composed them. Hence, he's known as the Father of English Hymnody.
- Because he was a nonconformist, Watts couldn't study at Oxford or Cambridge. Instead he went in 1690 at the age of 16 to the Dissenting Academy at Stoke Newington, which was then a village east of London. What makes Watts' hymns unique is his ability both to affirm central tenets of the Christian faith and to articulate how those convictions move the believer both in action and in soul.

'Come let us join our cheerful songs'

- Watts here sets words from Revelation 5 and transforms the account by inviting human beings to become part of the heavenly throng. Our human praise is transcended by the angels' heavenly contemplation.

Hymn: 'Come let us join our cheerful songs' (Nativity)

Three anthems

- Cecilia McDowell's setting of Watts' Cradle hymn was first performed in 2019. Its tender harmonies add to the sense of gentle rocking throughout. The hymn was first published in his 1706 book *Moral Songs*, at the conclusion of 'these Songs for Children'.
- In 'Give us the wings of faith', Isaac Watts took the Hebrews 6 description of the veil that shields heaven from our earthly eyes, and turned it into a fervent prayer that we might be given the wings of faith to rise within that veil and see the life of the saints who once dwelt as we do with sins and doubts and fears but now are surrounded by joys and glories. He then turns from intercession to

imagination, as he depicts himself asking the blessed ones whence cometh their victory – and the saints with one accord attribute it to Christ's sacrifice as the Lamb of God. Finally, he turns again, this time to preach and call on the singer to follow in Christ's footsteps. What's fascinating about this hymn is that Watts makes the ingredients of his parents' Puritan faith the constituents of a universal gospel: those ingredients are tribulation, walking with Christ, zeal, and victory.

- 'When I survey the wondrous cross' is Isaac Watts's best-known hymn. This is not so much a hymn about what Christ achieved on the cross, as about how his example changes our own lives. The words 'me', 'my' and 'I' occur 12 times in 16 lines. One of the most poignant lines is 'did e'er such love and sorrow meet'. The cross is the very extreme of sorrow but also the very extreme of love. Christianity is the recognition that true love must face untold sorrow if it is to be embodied in everlasting companionship.

Choir: 'Lo! He slumbers in his manger' – Cecilia McDowall (OUP)
Choir: 'Give us the wings of faith' – Ernest Bullock (OUP)
Choir: 'When I survey the wondrous cross' (from *St John Passion*) – Bob Chilcott (OUP)

'Jesus shall reign, where'er the sun'

- Isaac Watts seems not to fall into the traps many other writers do. Unlike some contemporary songwriters, he doesn't just focus on 'me and my feelings'. Unlike some Victorian writers, he doesn't collapse the gospel into social improvement. And in this hymn he speaks of the universality of the gospel without falling into a colonial mindset.
- He looks forward to a day when Jesus' kingdom stretches from shore to shore, until there is endless day, and prayer is continuous, and those of every tongue sing in sweet harmony, and prisoners, the weary and the suffering are transported to comfort, light and peace. It's a comprehensive vision, but it's clearly about God, not about our own aggrandisement, and it doesn't have any illusions about recasting God's kingdom in our own image.

Hymn: 'Jesus shall reign, where'er the sun' (Truro)

'Alas and did my Saviour bleed'

- When Isaac Watts complained to his father about the dreariness of singing existing hymns, his father challenged him to do better. It was one of the most significant conversations in the history of hymnody. In the following week a teenaged Isaac presented his first hymn, 'Behold the glories of the Lamb', to the church. A further 750 followed.

- This hymn expresses the grief of the believer at the suffering of Christ. The final line of the first stanza originally read 'For such a worm as I.'

Choir: 'Alas and did my Saviour bleed' – Stan Pethel (Hope Publishing Company)

William Blake

Choir: 'Songs in the night' – Victor Johnson (Choristers Guild)

William Blake (1757–1827)

- Blake was largely disregarded in his lifetime – but was voted by the public in 2002 as the 38th greatest Briton. He was baptized at St James's Piccadilly, and lived in London. He regarded himself as a Christian but was fiercely critical of the Church of England. As an artist and a poet, he was described thus by William Rossetti: 'a man not forestalled by predecessors, nor to be classed with contemporaries, nor to be replaced by known or readily surmisable successors'.

'To mercy, pity, peace, and love'

- For Blake, God is mercy, pity, peace and love: they are also the highest aspirations of humanity. Jesus Christ is the meeting place of the highest human aspirations and God's reality. Hence the name the Divine Image – God in us, but especially Jesus Christ as the image of God humanity fully alive.

Hymn: 'To mercy, pity, peace, and love' (Epsom)

Three anthems

- 'The Lamb' is all about simplicity. It is full of scriptural resonance, in its reference to the shepherd and the Lamb of God. There are echoes of the ram of Genesis 22, the sheep of Psalm 23 and Luke 15, and the good shepherd of John 10. The paradox is that the Lamb made the lamb. Tavener keeps this simplicity and poignancy throughout.
- 'Blake's Lullaby' was written in aid of Macmillan Cancer Support. The mood and the music are pervaded by loving peacefulness. But there are hints of threat, indicated by bold harmonic touches.

- Judith Weir was the first female Master of the Queen's Music. She draws on sources from medieval history, as well as the traditional stories and music of Scotland. She turned 'My guardian angel' by William Blake into a carol in which congregations sometimes sing the Alleluias.

Choir: 'The Lamb' – John Tavener (Chester Music)
Choir: 'Blake's Lullaby' – John Rutter (OUP)
Choir: 'My guardian angel' – Judith Weir (Chester Music)

'And did those feet in ancient time'

- This is a four-stanza poem from the preface to Blake's epic 'Milton: A Poem'. It is inspired by the apocryphal story that a young Jesus, accompanied by Joseph of Arimathea, a tin merchant, travelled to what is now England and visited Glastonbury during his unknown years. The poem suggests a visit by Jesus would briefly create heaven in England, in contrast to the 'dark Satanic mills' of the Industrial Revolution. Blake asks four questions rather than asserting a historical event: Did those feet walk? Was the holy lamb of God seen? Did the countenance shine forth? And, Was Jerusalem builded?
- Robert Bridges discovered the poem in 1916 and asked Hubert Parry to compose the tune. Parry turned it into a two-stanza hymn. It quickly became the Women's Suffrage hymn, and was consequently adopted by the Women's Institutes.

Hymn: 'And did those feet in ancient time' (Jerusalem)

'Tyger'

- This poem occupies the same place in Blake's collection *Songs of Experience* that 'The Lamb' does in *Songs of Innocence*: one is a poem about innocence, the other about primal ferocity. Both poems have the same pattern of questions and alliteration. Life, for Blake, is about holding contraries together.
- The first stanza asks, 'What immortal hand or eye / Could frame thy fearful symmetry?' The second stanza questions the Tyger about where he was created; the third queries how the creator formed him; the fourth explores what tools were used. In the fifth stanza, Blake wonders how the creator reacted to the Tyger, and who created the creature: which leads to the central question, Did he who made the Lamb make thee? Finally, the sixth stanza restates the central question while raising the stakes: rather than merely question what/who *could* create the Tyger, the speaker wonders: who *dares*.

Choir: 'Tyger' – Elaine Hagenberg (Elaine Hagenberg Music)

Cecil Frances Alexander

Choir: 'He is risen' – Percy Whitlock (OUP)

Cecil Frances Alexander (1818–95)

- Cecil Frances Humphreys was born in Dublin in 1818. As a young adult member of the Church of Ireland she came under the influence of the Oxford Movement, and especially John Keble, who fostered in her an Anglo-Catholic sacramental spirituality. In 1848 at the age of 30 she published *Hymns for Little Children* which went through no fewer than 69 editions before the end of the century. It contained what were to become some of her most famous and enduring hymns, including 'All things bright and beautiful', 'There is a green hill far away' and 'Once in royal David's city'.
- She used the profits from her celebrated hymn book to support the Derry and Raphoe Diocesan Institution for the Deaf and Dumb in Strabane. She was also involved with the Derry Home for Fallen Women, and worked to develop a district nurse service.
- She caused consternation in her family by taking up with and marrying William Alexander, a Church of Ireland clergyman and poet, who was six years her junior. Hence the name by which she is better known, Mrs C. F. Alexander. William went on to become Bishop of Derry and Archbishop of Armagh in 1867, only adding to his wife's fame.

'Jesus calls us; o'er the tumult'

- Mrs Alexander described the calling of the first disciples in her hymn 'Jesus calls us o'er the tumult'. It was written for St Andrew's Day and has her characteristic style of calling us to imitate the great figures of the Bible. We must set aside the things of the world and put Jesus above all things.

Hymn: 'Jesus calls us; o'er the tumult' (Saint Andrew)

Three anthems

- Cecil Frances had no children of her own, but took seriously her responsibilities as a godparent. She wrote hymns for each article of the Apostles' Creed in response to her godchildren's questioning, and these became some of her best-known works.

- The second article of the creed, 'who was conceived by the Holy Spirit, born of the Virgin Mary', became 'Once in royal David's city'. It locates the incarnation between creation and the second coming of Christ, and draws somewhat dated moral conclusions from Jesus' obedient childhood.
- Will Todd is a contemporary composer from County Durham, best known for his Mass in Blue.
- 'There is a green hill far away' is Mrs Alexander's meditation on the cross. Here she sums up the traditional Christian view of the atonement (without favouring any one specific theory) in the words, 'He died that we might be forgiven, he died to make us good, that we might go at last to heaven, saved by his precious blood.' But perhaps closer to the heart of Victorian spirituality is the final verse, 'O dearly, dearly has he loved! And we must love him too, and trust in his redeeming blood, and try his works to do.' Here again we find Mrs Alexander's insistence on moral example as the heart of Christianity. Bob Chilcott's St John Passion is an hour-long work telling the story of Christ's trial and crucifixion. It was written for Wells Cathedral in 2013. It includes four meditations taken from English poems from the thirteenth to the seventeenth centuries and five Passiontide hymns designed to be sung by choir and congregation together.
- The opening clauses of the Apostles' Creed, 'I believe in God the Father Almighty, Creator of heaven and earth', became 'All things bright and beautiful'. Today we love the purple headed mountain. But the original also contained the more controversial verse, 'The rich man in his castle, the poor man at his gate, God made them high and lowly, And ordered their estate', again illustrating how tied the author was to the social expectations of her era.

Choir: 'Once in royal David's city' – arr. Will Todd (Boosey & Hawkes)
Choir: 'There is a green hill far away' (from *St John Passion*) – Bob Chilcott (OUP)
Choir: 'All things bright and beautiful' – John Rutter (OUP)

'I bind unto myself today'

- One of Cecil Frances' great legacies is her translation of St Patrick's Breastplate, words probably written in the eighth century but attributed to St Patrick during his work in Ireland in the fifth century. H. H. Dickinson, Dean of the Chapel Royal at Dublin Castle, says, 'I wrote to her suggesting that she should fill a gap in our Irish Church Hymnal by giving us a metrical version of St. Patrick's "Lorica" [or breastplate] and I sent her a carefully collated copy of the best prose translations of it. Within a week she sent me that exquisitely beautiful as well as faithful version which appears in the appendix to our Church Hymnal.'
- The translation was set to music by Charles Villiers Stanford, an Irish composer, music teacher and conductor from Dublin. He was appointed organist at Trinity College, Cambridge, and at the age of 29 was one of the founding professors

of the Royal College of Music, where he taught composition. He was later Professor of Music at Cambridge. Among his pupils were Gustav Holst and Ralph Vaughan Williams.

Hymn: 'I bind unto myself today' (Saint Patrick)

'A prayer of St Patrick'

- John Rutter takes part of St Patrick's Breastplate, the words 'Christ be with me, Christ within me'. When Patrick was about 16, he was captured by Irish pirates from his home in Great Britain, and taken as a slave to Ireland, looking after animals, where he lived for six years before escaping and returning to his family. After becoming a priest, he returned to northern and western Ireland.
- The words of this anthem sum up the prayer that Christ become the believer's habitation and home. The connection with clothing makes this a perfect anthem for a baptism, particularly for the moment when the new Christian is clothed on emerging from the water.

Choir: 'A prayer of St Patrick' – John Rutter (OUP)

John Henry Newman

Choir: 'They are at rest' – Edward Elgar (public domain, published by OUP)

John Henry Newman (1801–90)

- Newman was born in 1801 and experienced a profound evangelical conversion at the age of 15. This nearly coincided with the banking crash that deeply affected his father. These two events left a significant mark on Newman's character. Despite breaking down in his final exams and doing poorly, he nonetheless came to be elected as a fellow at Oriel College, Oxford in 1822, where he was joined by E. B. Pusey a year later, and R. H. Froude in 1826. Newman became Vicar of the University Church in 1828. After John Keble inaugurated the Oxford Movement in 1833, Newman began to publish *Tracts for the Times*, which made him a national figure. In 1842 he retreated to Littlemore on the edge of Oxford and created a community there. He was received into the Roman Catholic Church in 1845 – a seismic event in the still virulently anti-Catholic Church of England.

- Newman's life as a Roman Catholic is less well known. He became Rector of University College, Dublin in 1854, during which time he wrote *The Idea of a University*. In 1864, in response to criticism from Charles Kingsley, he published *Apologia Pro Vita Sua*, explaining the decisions he'd made on his path to Catholicism. He opposed the declaration of papal infallibility in 1870, and became a cardinal in 1879. He died in 1890, and was canonized in 2019. He was one of the great English men of letters of his century.

'Firmly I believe and truly'

- Newman published *The Dream of Gerontius* in 1865. It is a Dante-like journey of the soul to God through purgatory and paradise. At one point the little old man Gerontius asks for a period of cleansing lest his sin besmirch the purity of God. The poem was set by Elgar in 1900 in his finest choral work, and this section was first used as a hymn in the *English Hymnal* in 1906. The hymn is a summary of Gerontius' faith, covering Trinity, Incarnation, Cross and the Catholic Church like a creed.

Hymn: 'Firmly I believe and truly' (Shipston)

Three anthems

- 'Be merciful, be gracious' is one part of Elgar's setting of *The Dream of Gerontius*. Writing about death and the life beyond were almost unknown in Newman's time, and there was much speculation about his motivation and sources. It became very influential and remains a key text in Victorian literature about death.
- 'Lead, kindly Light' is an 1833 poem entitled 'The Pillar of Cloud', referring to the guidance given to the children of Israel as they left Egypt during the exodus. It was among the hymns published in Newman's *Lyra Apostolica*. Newman became ill while in Italy and was unable to travel: he later said, 'We were becalmed for whole week in the Straits of Bonifacio, and it was there that I wrote the lines, Lead, kindly Light.' On Tuesday 16 February 1909 at West Stanley Colliery, 168 men and boys lost their lives as the result of two underground explosions. Incredibly, there were still men alive underground. A group of 34 men and boys had found a pocket of clean air. Some panicked and left the group, dying instantly after inhaling poison gas. The remainder sat in almost total darkness, when one of them began humming the hymn 'Lead kindly Light'. The rest of the miners joined in with the words, 'Lead, kindly Light amidst the encircling gloom, lead thou me on / The night is dark, and I am far away from home'. These 26 men were rescued after 14 hours. Four others were later rescued.

- 'Solitude' is a setting of a poem Newman wrote in 1818 while still an undergraduate. James Whitbourn's arrangement was commissioned by Oriel College, Oxford, where Newman was a fellow from 1822 until 1845, and it was first performed in 2019, coinciding with Newman's canonization. Solitude was a recurring theme in his writing. James Whitbourn died in 2024.

Choir: 'Be merciful, be gracious' (from *The Dream of Gerontius*) – Edward Elgar (Novello)
Choir: 'Lead, kindly Light' (from *Eternal Light: A Requiem*) – Howard Goodall (Faber Music)
Choir: 'Solitude' – James Whitbourn (OUP)

'Praise to the holiest in the height'

- This is yet another excerpt from *The Dream of Gerontius*. It was first used as a hymn in the 1868 Appendix to *Hymns Ancient & Modern*. It is a six-verse exposition of the notion of the *felix culpa* – the idea, tracing back to St Ambrose and included in the liturgy of the Easter Vigil, that Adam's fault was a happy one because it led to so great a salvation as that provided in Jesus.
- The reference to a higher gift than grace refers not to the doctrine of transubstantiation but to the incarnate Christ. The stirring words 'In man for man' offer a four-word summary of Christology and the atonement.

Hymn: 'Praise to the holiest in the height' (Gerontius)

'Littlemore tractus'

- This piece was commissioned in 1999 so its first performance in February 2001 would coincide with the 200th anniversary of Newman's birth. The words come from a sermon Newman preached in 1843 while Vicar of Littlemore. The sermon ends, 'May he support us all the day long, till the shades lengthen, and the evening comes, and the busy world is hushed, and the fever of life is over, and our work is done! Then in his mercy may he give us a safe lodging, and a holy rest, and peace at the last.' These words are often used at funerals and in evening services. The sermon was a meditation on Matthew 10.16, 'Behold, I send you forth as sheep in the midst of wolves; be ye therefore as wise as serpents, and as harmless as doves.' The first performance of Pärt's anthem was in Littlemore Church by the Choir of St Martin-in-the-Fields.

Choir: 'Littlemore tractus' – Arvo Pärt (Universal Edition)

Gerard Manley Hopkins

Choir: 'Heaven-Haven' – Samuel Barber (Schirmer)

Gerard Manley Hopkins (1844–89)

- If Robert Bridges had not started publishing some of Gerard Manley Hopkins' poems after the latter's death in 1889, the world would never have heard of one of the most highly regarded and influential poets of the modern era. Hopkins was baptized an Anglican, but became a Roman Catholic while at Oxford, at a time when that often involved estrangement from one's family. He soon felt a call to become a Jesuit priest. After years of struggle, which involved him burning his poems, he was eventually inspired by reading the medieval philosopher Duns Scotus to realize that faith and poetry need not conflict. Eventually he was so transfixed by the created world that he sketched, wrote poems and composed music. In 1884 he became Professor of Classics at University College, Dublin, but he felt out of sympathy with the growing Irish Republicanism of Catholics at the time. He died of typhoid five years later in Dublin at the age of 44.
- Hopkins' poetry is unique. This comes partly from its rhythm, influenced by the Welsh language and by Old English verse such as Beowulf. Hopkins also developed, partly from Duns Scotus, the notion of inscape, which has been described as 'the charged essence, the absolute singularity that gives each created thing its being; instress is both the energy that holds the inscape together and the process by which this inscape is perceived by an observer.' This is what gives his nature poems such vigour.

'Godhead here in hiding'

- This is a translation by Gerard Manley Hopkins of Thomas Aquinas' hymn '*Adoro te devote*'. It begins, 'Godhead here in hiding whom I do adore / Masked by these bare shadows, shape and nothing more.' The hymn is a meditation of the doctrine of transubstantiation, by which the nature, or substance, of bread and wine change into the body and blood of Christ, while the accidents, or physical characteristics, remain the same. Thus Jesus is as perfectly present in the Eucharist as he is in heaven.

Hymn: 'Godhead here in hiding' (Adoro te devote)

Gerard Manley Hopkins

Three anthems

- 'Moonless darkness' is a Christmas poem in which Hopkins explores new beginnings. The sun rises. Jesus is a new era for the world and a new way of understanding God's presence. Most of all, Christmas is full of possibility for a new beginning for the poet himself. Hopkins is evidently struggling with his own shortcomings, and his prayers are simple: 'Make me pure, Lord: Thou art holy; Make me meek, Lord: Thou wert lowly.' Here these words are set by the American early twentieth-century composer Amy Beach.
- 'God's Grandeur' is Hopkins' fulsome celebration of the irrepressible magnificence of God in creation. He enjoys, in characteristic style, the way that grandeur 'will flame out, like shining from shook foil' and how it 'gathers to a greatness, like the ooze of oil / Crushed.' Even though 'Generations have trod, have trod, have trod', for all this 'nature is never spent', because, thrillingly, 'There lives the dearest freshness deep down things'. And why? In a reference to the Genesis 1 creation story, Hopkins asserts, 'Because the Holy Ghost over the bent / World broods.' Kenneth Leighton was a mid-twentieth-century composer raised, unlike many composers, in humble working-class Wakefield. He taught James MacMillan among other distinguished students at Edinburgh.
- 'Pied Beauty' was written in 1877 and published in 1918 with several other of Hopkins' poems by Robert Bridges. It's a celebration of what Hopkins calls dappled things – notably trout, with their spotted complexion, together with cattle and finches, and ultimately the landscape as a whole. The crescendo of this endless variety and creativity in creation contrasts with the changeless creator, the very opposite of creation. Hopkins makes this poem a hymn of praise from the overflowing diversity of creation to the wondrous simplicity of God. Here's a setting by Paul Spicer, a contemporary conductor and student of Herbert Howells.

Choir: 'Moonless darkness' – Amy Beach (Encore Publications)
Choir: 'God's Grandeur' – Kenneth Leighton (Novello)
Choir: 'Glory be to God for dappled things' – Paul Spicer (Boosey & Hawkes)

'The word of God proceeding forth'

- 'The word of God proceeding forth' is a translation by Hopkins of Thomas Aquinas' hymn '*Verbum Supernum*' composed for Corpus Christi. The feast of Corpus Christi, celebrated on the Thursday after Trinity Sunday, was originally proposed to the Pope by Thomas Aquinas in 1264, the year after he wrote this hymn.

Hymn: 'The word of God proceeding forth' (Wareham)

'The spring of the water of life'

- Commissioned by Wilshire Baptist Church in Dallas, Texas, to mark the 30th anniversary of Senior Pastor George A. Mason, this jubilant anthem sets Gerard Manley Hopkins' 'God's Grandeur' and George Herbert's 'The Flower', together with words from Revelation, culminating in a triumphant finale. Howard Goodall is a composer of music for liturgical singing, stage musicals and film and television screens.

Choir: 'The spring of the water of life' – Howard Goodall (MorningStar Music Publishers)

Robert Bridges

Choir: 'My eyes for beauty pine' – Herbert Howells (Novello)

Robert Bridges (1844–1930)

- Robert Bridges was Britain's poet laureate from 1913 to 1930. His poems reflect a deep Christian faith. Many have been used for hymns, including 'O gladsome light'. He was born in Kent and was educated at Eton. He went on to study medicine at St Bartholomew's Hospital and practised at several different hospitals. He became ill with pneumonia, forcing him to retire in 1882, at which point he devoted himself to writing and literary research. He was associated with many notable musicians, such as Stainer, Stanford, Parry and Holst.
- Bridges was a key figure in English hymnody. He found congregational singing appropriate to express faith, celebration and fellowship. But hymns of lament, humiliation, repentance, divine affection and similar emotions, he believed to be more appropriate for singing by a choir only. For his ideal hymn book, he listed categories of music in chronological order. Plainsong took pride of place. He lived in the Berkshire village of Yattendon, where he directed the church choir, and in 1899 published the *Yattendon Hymnal*, a key precursor to the *English Hymnal* of 1906.

'Happy are they, they that love God'

- This is a translation made by Robert Bridges of a hymn written in Latin by the French author and Rector of the University of Paris (now known as the

Sorbonne), Charles Coffin. The hymn is about the joyful unity of those who dwell together in Christ. Bridges changes the location of the original hymn to be now not so much centred on the Church as on the blessed Christian home. The hymn finishes with the trust that God can use even our sorrows for good and to lead us closer to Christ.

Hymn: 'Happy are they, they that love God' (Binchester)

Three anthems

- 'Jesu, joy of man's desiring' began life as a chorale in J. S. Bach's 1723 Advent Cantata. The English title derives from piano transcriptions made by Myra Hess, in 1926 for piano solo and in 1934 for piano duet. The words were written by the German pastor Martin Janus in 1661 and were commonly sung to a Johann Schop melody. The translation made by Robert Bridges was from the original Martin Janus hymn, not from the version used in Bach's cantata. Whereas Janus' original was a stirring and exuberant praise hymn, Bridges' version is a gentler, more intimate version.
- 'Christ hath a garden' was originally written by Isaac Watts and edited by Robert Bridges. It intriguingly plays with the notion of a garden as the setting of Eden but also of paradise, and traces how Christ takes the spirit of the first in opening the way to the second. Today the hymn has a third dimension when sung in the context of the ecological crisis and the notion of the world as Christ's garden. Eleanor Daley is a Canadian composer based in Ontario.
- Judith Weir is the first female Master of the Queen's Music. She often draws on sources from medieval history, as well as the traditional stories and music of Scotland. Robert Bridges' 'I love all beauteous things' contrasts God's creation, which lasts, and ours, which doesn't. But it suggests we can still come closest to God when we seek beauty by making things.

Choir: 'Jesu, joy of man's desiring' – Johann Sebastian Bach (public domain, published by RSCM and others)
Choir: 'Christ hath a garden' – Eleanor Daley (OUP)
Choir: 'I love all beauteous things' – Judith Weir (Chester)

'All my hope on God is founded'

- Joachim Neander was a seventeenth-century German Calvinist. He was on the brink of death, at the tender age of 30, when he wrote the famous words 'All my hope on God is founded'. Two hundred and fifty years later, almost to the day, Robert Bridges translated Neander's hymn and sent it to Herbert Howells. Howells was deep in grief after the death from spinal meningitis of his nine-year-old son Michael. He received the hymn text at breakfast time, and he didn't move from his chair until he'd composed this tune. He named the tune 'Michael'.

Hymn: 'All my hope on God is founded' (Michael)

'Haste on, my joys'

- The sixth of Gerald Finzi's Seven Poems of Robert Bridges, a 20-minute unaccompanied setting of lyrical poetry, including in some of the finest part songs of their period. 'Haste on, my joys' has a distinctive lightness of touch, without some of the melancholy found elsewhere.

Choir: 'Haste on, my joys' – Gerald Finzi (OUP)

Contemporary hymnwriters

Hymns

- Christian hymns are rooted in the praise of Israel expressed by the psalms. Early surviving Christian hymns, such as 'Hail gladdening light', retain the character of Old Testament hymns. Hymns got great encouragement from the conversion of Constantine and the much freer ability to worship in the fourth century. Eastern Christianity had a greater range and versatility than the West, and Ephraim the Syrian, who lived at this time, is seen as the originator of a distinctively Christian style. In the West, Hilary of Poitiers and Ambrose of Milan were significant figures in advancing congregational singing. By the Middle Ages choral ensembles had largely displaced congregational singing, but in the Reformation congregations made a comeback. Martin Luther was among those who harnessed secular movements in music to ecclesial effect, and Pietism was a major influence in German-speaking Christianity from the seventeenth century onwards.
- Calvinism was suspicious of singing anything besides metrical settings of the psalms; it took the prodigious work of Isaac Watts in England to transform the imagination of worship and accept the theologically shaped and scripturally doused emerging tradition of hymnody. Charles Wesley then took hymns to a wider public and a new dimension. The Church of England took till the 1820s fully to embrace the singing of hymns, which was hitherto looked down upon as a nonconformist practice. After World War Two there was a generation of hymnwriters eager to adapt the Christian imagination to the modern world;

meanwhile, the charismatic revival of the late twentieth century produced an outpouring of choruses. The two traditions have often overlapped in vigorous and generative ways.

'Earth's fragile beauties we possess'

- Robert Willis, Dean of Canterbury from 2001 to 2022, here sees the life of discipleship as a pilgrimage. He is particularly fascinated by the children of Israel's experience in the wilderness. Famine, plague and sword triggered the exodus, but once across the Red Sea, trials were not over. The hymn is a lament, facing up to sorrow and suffering with faith, hope and love. The ultimate inspiration is Christ crucified – seen in 'wounded feet', 'wounded hands', and 'wounded heart'. Vaughan Williams' tune 'Kingsfold' suits the blend of aching grief and abiding trust.

Hymn: 'Earth's fragile beauties we possess' (Kingsfold)

Three anthems

- Stuart Townend is a leading contemporary hymnwriter, whose fresh and tuneful pieces such as 'In Christ alone' and 'How deep the Father's love' have kept alive traditions of conventional hymns in the realms of evangelical piety. His compositions have an uncompromising insistence on penal substitutionary understandings of the atonement. Here he adapts the ancient theme of St Patrick's Breastplate to perceive Christ in all the moods and activities of the day. The original words, both those that begin 'I bind unto myself today' and those that divert to 'Christ be with me', were probably written in the eighth century but are invariably attributed to St Patrick during his work in Ireland in the fifth century.
- Bernadette Farrell is a community organizer and liturgical specialist. Born in Yorkshire, she has spent many years in London as perhaps the leading Catholic hymnwriter of her generation. Her hymns 'O God, you search me and you know me' and 'Christ be our light' are among the best known of all contemporary hymns. Her 1983 hymn 'Unless a grain of wheat' is a meditation on John's Gospel, taking themes that speak of Jesus' sacrificial call on all disciples.
- In 'Hymns, psalms and sacred songs', Thomas Hewitt Jones sets a hymn by Timothy Dudley-Smith, whose influence on contemporary British hymnody is immeasurable. The specific reference to hymns and psalms and sacred songs comes in Ephesians 5.19 and Colossians 3.16.

Choir: 'Christ be in my waking' – Stuart Townend (multiple hymn books)
Choir: 'Unless a grain of wheat' – Bernadette Farrell (OCP)
Choir: 'Hymns, psalms and sacred songs' – Thomas Hewitt Jones (RSCM)

'Hope of our calling'

- This is a hymn from one of the most prolific and prophetic hymnwriters working today. Ally Barrett is Associate Vicar of Great St Mary's in Cambridge. She is also an accomplished preacher and liturgist, with experience in training clergy for ordination. This hymn is a powerful assertion of the nature of vocation, which was influential on the movement for the ordination of women as bishops.

Hymn: 'Hope of our calling' (Woodlands)

'Cloth for the cradle'

- Perhaps no one in Britain has had a greater influence on contemporary hymn writing than John Bell. Like many of his hymns, this originates in a Scottish folk tune, in this case 'Wae's me for Prince Charlie'. Here he takes the swaddling clothes wrapped around the baby Jesus as the pretext for finding a 'shawl that's woven by us all'. The verses each introduce us to the panoply of characters that have a part in the tapestry of this holy cloth: claimant and queen, wage earners in between, hungry and poor, the sick and the unsure, wrinkled or fair, carefree or full of care. Bell is never afraid to take a risk with a lyric in order to keep the gospel's social and theological edge; but he is rigorous in ensuring every hymn is tried for years before being published, so all his work is thoroughly road-tested.

Choir: 'Cloth for the cradle' – John Bell (GIA Publications)

SAINTS

Choir: 'Hail glorious spirits, heirs of light' – Christopher Tye (public domain)

Michael

- St Michael was the protector of Israel in the book of Daniel. In Revelation Michael and the angels fight against the dragon and his angels. Jude refers to Michael as the archangel fighting the devil. Basil the Great in the fifth century designated Michael the primary archangel. In Roman Catholicism Michael has four roles. He is the leader of heaven's forces in their triumph over the powers of hell; he is the angel of death, carrying the souls of all the deceased to heaven and giving each soul the chance to redeem itself before passing; he weighs souls in his perfectly balanced scales; and he is guardian of the Church, while being patron saint of a number of cities and countries. St Michael is not to be confused with the trademark of Marks and Spencer, which honours Michael Marks, the co-founder.
- In Christianity, angels are fundamentally messengers. Thus they are a way of preserving God's holiness, yet drawing close to humankind. The New Testament has not fully adjusted to the full implications of the incarnation in finding a different way to overcome this problem. Thus there is always a danger with angels that they assume a unitarian God and do the work that within the Trinity belongs to Jesus and the Holy Spirit. In particular, angels today are more or less a synonym for the Holy Spirit.

'Christ, the fair glory of the holy angels'

- This hymn was written by Rabanus Maurus (*c.* 776–856) who was born of noble parents at Mainz. In 803, he became director of the school at the Benedictine Abbey at Fulda. After a pilgrimage to Palestine, in 822 he became Abbott at Fulda, retiring in 842. In 847, he became Archbishop of Mainz. He wrote extensive biblical commentaries, and other works which were widely read in the Middle Ages. He also wrote 'Come, Holy Ghost, our souls inspire'.

- The hymn was translated by Percy Dearmer, long-time Vicar of St Mary's, Primrose Hill in London, author of *The Parson's Handbook*, 1899, and one of the compilers of the *English Hymnal*, 1906. He wrote 'A brighter dawn is breaking' and 'Jesu, good above all other'.

Hymn: 'Christ, the fair glory of the holy angels' (Christe Sanctorum)

Three anthems

- 'For he shall give his angels' forms the seventh section of the first part of Felix Mendelssohn's oratorio *Elijah*. The words, which come from Psalm 91, are quoted by the Devil in the temptation narrative to persuade Jesus to jump from the pinnacle of the Temple in Jerusalem. Mendelssohn's work premiered in 1846. It describes events in Elijah's life and intersperses celebratory psalms. This is the original a capella version of the well-known chorus.
- John Tavener's 'Song for Athene' is taken from words by Mother Thekla, an Orthodox nun and spiritual director to Tavener, who lived in Whitby, Yorkshire. Tavener wrote the anthem in 1993 as a tribute to Athene Hariades, a young half-Greek actress and a family friend who was killed in a cycling accident. Contrary to some assumptions, the name Athene is thus not a direct reference to the mythological Greek goddess. The anthem is famous as being sung for the recession of the coffin at Princess Diana's funeral, in perhaps the most mesmerizing liturgical moment in Church of England funeral services in the twentieth century.
- '*In paradisum*' is an antiphon from the traditional Latin Requiem liturgy. It is traditionally sung by the choir as the body is being taken out of the church. The text is: 'May the angels lead you into paradise; may the martyrs receive you at your arrival, and lead you to the holy city Jerusalem. May choirs of angels receive you and with Lazarus, once a poor man, may you have eternal rest.' Gabriel Fauré composed his *Requiem* between 1887 and 1890. It is the best-known of his large works. It asserts eternal rest and consolation.

Choir: 'For he shall give his angels' – Felix Mendelssohn (Church Music Society)
Choir: 'Song for Athene' – John Tavener (Chester Music)
Choir: In paradisum (from *Requiem*) – Gabriel Fauré (public domain, published by Oxford University Press)

'Ye watchers and ye holy ones'

- This hymn was written for the *English Hymnal* of 1906 by one of its compilers, Athelstan Riley. A sixth-century account by the theologian known as Pseudo-Dionysius ordered the heavenly places in threes: cherubim, seraphim and thrones; dominations, virtues and powers; principalities, archangels and angels. Riley fits all of these into the first verse of his hymn, but then interestingly places Mary ('bearer of the eternal word') above them all. Then he brings in the patriarchs, prophets and worshippers on earth. The seventeenth-century German tune, best known for accompanying 'All creatures of our God and king', was arranged by Ralph Vaughan Williams for the *English Hymnal*.

Hymn: 'Ye watchers and ye holy ones' (Lasst uns erfreuen)

'*Factum est silentium*'

- One glorious moral use of the notion of angels is made by Thomas Traherne, in his *Centuries of Meditations* 2:68: 'Suppose a curious and fair woman. Some have seen the beauties of Heaven in such a person. It is a vain thing to say they loved too much. I dare say there are ten thousand beauties in that creature which they have not seen: They loved it not too much, but upon false causes. Nor so much upon false ones, as only upon some little ones. They love a creature for sparkling eyes and curled hair … which they should love moreover for being God's Image, Queen of the Universe, beloved by Angels, redeemed by Jesus Christ, an heiress of Heaven, and temple of the Holy Ghost. They love her perhaps, but do not love God more: nor men as much: nor Heaven and Earth at all … We should be all Life and Mettle and Vigour and Love to everything; and that would poise us. I dare confidently say that every person in the whole world ought to be beloved as much as this … But God being beloved infinitely more, will be infinitely more our joy, and our heart will be more with Him, so that no man can be in danger by loving others too much, that loveth God as he ought.'
- In this anthem, the early-seventeenth-century composer Richard Dering portrays the violent clashes of the book of Revelation: 'There was silence in heaven while the dragon fought with the Archangel Michael. A sound was heard, thousands of thousands saying: salvation, honour and power to almighty God. Alleluia.' It is hard not to draw a parallel with the bloodthirstiness of the Reformation in Dering's own time.

Choir: *Factum est silentium* – Richard Dering (public domain, published in *The Oxford Book of Tudor Anthems*, OUP)

St Francis of Assisi

Choir: 'All creatures of our God and King' – William Harris (RSCM)

Theme

- St Francis of Assisi is perhaps the most instantly recognizable and lovable of all the saints of the Church. Francis was born in Assisi in central Italy in 1181. He had a complex relationship with his father. Rather than take over the family business he set off to fight against the neighbouring city of Perugia. He was captured and imprisoned. Through the humiliation of this experience, he started to realize his vocation to become an instrument of God's peace. He tried to give away his father's wealth to clothe the poor and, having renounced his possessions, stood naked in the town square.

'Make me a channel of your peace'

- The Prayer of St Francis of Assisi, sometimes known as the Peace Prayer or 'Make me a channel of your peace', wasn't written by St Francis in the twelfth century. It was written in 1912 by a French Catholic priest, Esther Bouquerel, and published in a small-circulation spiritual magazine. At the end of World War One, the French Franciscan Étienne Benoît printed millions of copies of the prayer on a card that depicted St Francis on the back.
- A few years later an English translation was printed in a Quaker magazine in the USA under the title 'A Prayer of St Francis of Assisi' – and the rest is history. By the time the South African third order Franciscan Sebastian Temple wrote 'Make me a channel of your peace' in 1967 all connection with historical attribution was long gone.

Hymn: 'Make me a channel of your peace' (Make me a channel)

Three anthems

- Francis began to see himself as the brother of the poor and of all creation. One day he saw a leper coming towards him along the path. Leprosy was the most feared sickness of his age. Yet he was drawn to embrace and kiss the leper. It was a moment that epitomized his emerging call to perceive God's presence in all living things.

- Francis, in his sense of creation as something to be befriended rather than subdued, was a prophet well ahead of his time. 'The canticle of Brother Sun', here set by long-time Magdalen College, Oxford organist Grayston Ives, was written by Francis, and is believed to be the first hymn or poem of praise recorded in Italian.
- The Benedicite constitutes an apocryphal addition to Daniel 3, comprising verses 35–65 in Catholic Bibles. It is sometimes known as the 'Song of the Three Children', since it is presented as Shadrach, Meshach and Abednego's hymn of praise on their deliverance from Nebuchadnezzar's fiery furnace. Francis Jackson, who died in 2022, was a long-time director of music at York Minster.
- Francis did not wish his followers to be exactly like him. His dying prayer, uttered as he lay on the dirt floor of a hut near his beloved Portiuncula chapel, was: 'I have done what is mine; may Christ teach you what is yours.' Lucy Walker is an award-winning composer, pianist and music educator based in Cambridge.

Choir: 'The canticle of Brother Sun' – Grayston Ives (OUP)
Choir: Benedicite in G – Francis Jackson (Banks Music Publications)
Choir: 'I have done what is mine to do' – Cecilia McDowall (Shorter House)

'All creatures of our God and King'

- One less well-known story of great contemporary significance about Francis is that he visited the Holy Land not as a crusader but to visit the Muslim Sultan. The two men spent a long time talking together. Francis did not abandon his love of Christ or his desire to convert this Muslim leader, but they came away with a deep understanding and respect for one another and a friendship and realization of a God far greater than and beyond their differences.
- For Francis, the incarnation was not just the historical event of God becoming one of us. The incarnation was then, but it is also now. Anyone who accepts the gospel life accepts the commission from God continually to bring forth Christ into our world. Francis put it this way: 'We are ... [his] mothers when we carry him in our heart and body through love and a pure and sincere conscience; and give him birth through a holy activity, which must shine before others by example.'
- 'All creatures of our God and King' captures his alignment with all creation in a chorus of praise.

Hymn: 'All creatures of our God and King' (Lass uns erfreuen)

'Lord, make me an instrument of thy peace'

- To get a full picture of Francis' significance for today, one must appreciate not just his poverty, nor his founding of what became a large and influential order of friars, nor his relationship to creation, but also his profound perception of peace.

Choir: 'Lord, make me an instrument of thy peace' – Rutter (RSCM)

St Luke

Choir: 'Be still for the presence of the Lord' – David Evans arr. Indra J. Hughes (Novello)

St Luke and healing

- Luke wrote Luke and Acts. Acts often uses the narrator's voice of 'we' so it seems the author of Acts was also the Luke who Paul calls the 'beloved physician' in Colossians 4.14. It is written in beautiful Greek and its elaborate prologue comes in seven sections, interweaving the stories of John the Baptist and Jesus. Luke has a particular interest in outcasts and women: he also records the most famous parables, of the Good Samaritan and the Prodigal Son. Luke's overall project, as Acts makes clear, is to commend Christianity to the Roman Empire. He does so through narrating Jesus' journey to Jerusalem and Paul's journey to Rome.
- Prayer for healing is controversial. That's because there are two contrasting traditions. The first, which we could call resurrection, is to plead with God for a miracle. Whether through brilliant doctors, an inexplicable halt in malady, or through the problem just evaporating, it's an impulse to will God into bringing life from the dead. The second way we could call incarnation. Whether a courageous attempt at dignified and stoic resignation or a faith-shaped conviction that Jesus is with us, this is a prayer that the sick be given strength and patience to last them through the frightening, perhaps painful and certainly distressing last months of their lives.
- But there is also a prayer that says, if this can't be happy, make it beautiful. It says make this season a time when the sick find a depth of love, companionship and truth they've never known before. As they stare down the intimidating frown of death, give them a richer sense of the wonder of living, a joyful thankfulness for what they've seen and known, an ability to bless others as they face

daunting challenges themselves, and a piercing insight into the heart of God. The word for this is transfiguration.

'Immortal love, forever full'

- Like the Quaker John Whittier's 'Dear Lord and Father', this hymn began life as part of a longer poem, 'Our Master', published in 1867. W. Garrett Horder brought the poem from the USA to the UK and published it in his *Congregational Hymns* in 1884. The hymn almost has a sense of a love that Jesus embodies in his life, ministry and passion – rather than that Jesus precisely is that love. Whittier sees hell as turning away from love, and heaven as walking with love. The tune 'Bishopthorpe' has been attributed to Jeremiah Clarke, the English baroque composer and organist, best known for his Trumpet Voluntary often played at weddings.

Hymn: 'Immortal love, forever full' (Bishopthorpe)

Three anthems

- Charlotte Elliott was the granddaughter of Henry Venn, one of the Clapham Sect around William Wilberforce. She was struck down with sickness aged 32 and it dogged her for her last 50 years of life. She wrote hundreds of hymns, and published them in *The Invalid's Hymn Book* and *Hours of Sorrow Cheered and Conforted*. She wrote 'Just as I am' as her brother Harry was raising funds to build a college in Brighton for daughters of poor clergy. Charlotte felt useless to help – but her hymn, written that day, proved far more influential than the bazaar. She recalled words spoken to her by a Swiss evangelist in 1822: he had said, 'Come to Jesus, just as you are.' William Wordsworth's daughter asked for the hymn to be read to her every morning as she approached death in Grasmere. Bob Chilcott has mastered the art of setting familiar words to new tunes – and this is among his finest.
- Salvation is the transformation of our past – the forgiveness of sins. And the promise of the future – eternal life. Healing is the third part of salvation, the part sandwiched between forgiveness and eternal life. This is what salvation means: there's forgiveness, there's eternal life and, in between, filling up any space that may linger between forgiveness and everlasting life, there's healing. William Harris took words from Isaiah 35 and placed them in a modern context in his celebrated anthem 'Strengthen ye the weak hands'.
- Thomas Hewitt Jones won the BBC Young Composer Competition in his teens, and he became well known for his Christmas piece, 'What Child is this?' His composition 'Funny song' was widely played internationally in 2022. 'A love

unfeigned' is a poem, which is also a prayer, on the theme of Good Friday, written by the British poet Geoffrey Dearmer (1893–1996), who was deeply affected by his experience of World War One. Geoffrey Dearmer was the son of Percy Dearmer, compiler of the *English Hymnal*.

Choir: 'Just as I am' – Bob Chilcott (OUP)
Choir: 'Strengthen ye the weak hands' – William Harris (Novello)
Choir: 'A love unfeigned' – Thomas Hewitt Jones (RSCM)

'We cannot measure how you heal'

- This hymn is inspired by the healings in the Gospels, such as the centurion's servant in Luke 7. John Bell describes how God's healing can occur in present struggles, in death, and in the lives of those that have not been born. He has great faith in the touch of friends. Like many of Bell's hymns, it is set to a Scottish folk tune.

Hymn: 'We cannot measure how you heal' (Ye banks and braes)

'It's me, O Lord'

- Michael Mosoeu Moerane is a Black South African choral composer, born near the border with Lesotho. 'It's me, O Lord' is one of eight African American spirituals he has arranged. It is in call-and-response style, led by the soprano.

Choir: 'It's me, O Lord' – Spiritual arr. Michael Moerane (African Composers Edition)

St Cecilia

Choir: 'Let all the world in every corner sing' – Greta Tomlins (Multitude of Voyces)

St Cecilia's Day

- St Cecilia's Day falls on 22 November. She has long been celebrated as the patron saint of music. She lived in the second or third century in Rome or Sicily. When the time came for her marriage to be consummated, Cecilia told her husband Valerian that she had an angel of the Lord watching over her who would

punish him if he dared to violate her virginity, but who would love him if he could respect her maidenhood. When Valerian asked to see the angel, Cecilia replied that he would see the angel if he would go to the third milestone on the Appian Way and be baptized by Pope Urban.
- Through her preaching she had by this time converted 400 people, whom Pope Urban forthwith baptized. Then Cecilia was arrested, and condemned to be suffocated in the baths. She was shut in for a night and a day, and the fires were heaped up, and made to glow and roar their utmost, but Cecilia did not even break out into perspiration through the heat. When the prefect Turcius Almachius heard this, he sent an executioner to cut off her head in the bath. The man struck three times without being able to sever the head from the trunk. He left her bleeding, and she lived three days. Crowds came to her, and collected her blood with napkins and sponges, while she preached to them or prayed. At the end of that period she died, and was buried by Pope Urban and his deacons.

'When in our music God is glorified'

- Fred Pratt Green started writing hymns in retirement and by the time he died had become the most prolific Methodist hymnwriter since Wesley. Charles Villiers Stanford's tune, written for 'For all the saints', had been superseded for those words by Sine Nomine, so Fred Pratt Green was asked to adopt the orphaned tune and write a new hymn to go with it.

Hymn: 'When in our music God is glorified' (Engelberg)

Three anthems

- William Byrd's setting of the first four verses of Psalm 81 is a paradoxical composition, because it is an exuberant celebration by choral singers of the music made by a range of instruments – the timbrel, the pleasant harp and the viol. In the psalm, the musical extravaganza marks a feast day, and is made a law of Israel and of God.
- The poem 'A hymn for St Cecilia' by Ursula Vaughan Williams (wife of Ralph) praises the patron saint of music. It was written for the Livery Club of the Worshipful Company of Musicians to mark Herbert Howells' Mastership of the Company in 1959. The Company once had control over all musical performance in the City. Ursula Vaughan Williams wrote, 'My St Cecilia is a girl in one of those magical gardens from Pompeian frescoes, a romantic figure among colonnades and fountains; Herbert's tune takes her briskly towards martyrdom.'

- James MacMillan's short anthem on texts from Psalm 96 includes inflections of Scottish folk music, Gaelic psalmody and plainsong, plus hints of the work of John Tavener. It has a powerful organ postlude.

Choir: 'Sing joyfully' – William Byrd (public domain, published in *The Oxford Book of Tudor Anthems*, OUP)
Choir: 'A hymn for St Cecilia' – Herbert Howells (Novello)
Choir: 'A new song' – James MacMillan (Boosey & Hawkes)

'How shall I sing that majesty'

- This is a magnificent hymn that speaks of the greatness of God and smallness of humanity. Its searching questions echo those of Samuel Crossman in 'My song is love unknown', written a little earlier in the seventeenth century. It blends themes from Psalms 104, about God's majesty, and 139, about God's tender concern for each one of us. John Mason (after whom the Victorian hymn translator John Mason Neale was named) explores how one as flawed as I could join the heavenly choir, and concludes that just as the widow offered her mite, so we can do the same to the angels. The peerless theology of the final verse is based on Augustine's assertion that God is an infinite circle whose centre is everywhere and whose circumference is nowhere. The tune, written in 1958, is named after a field in the centre of Cambridge onto which backs the Leys School, where the tune's composer Ken Naylor taught for many years.

Hymn: 'How shall I sing that majesty' (Coe Fen)

'How can I keep from singing?'

- This is an American folk song that began as a Christian hymn. The author of the lyrics was known only as 'Pauline T'. The tune was composed by American Baptist minister Robert Lowry. Today it is often sung in a secular version that advocates solidarity in the face of oppression. It was not originally a Quaker hymn; nonetheless, Quakers adopted it and use it widely today.
- Canadian composer and educator Sarah Quartel lives in London, Ontario. She grew up the daughter of a church organist, and recalls that she was eight years old before she realized that not everyone had a harpsichord in their basement. Here she gives the old song a thrilling a capella arrangement.

Choir: 'How can I keep from singing?' – Sarah Quartel (OUP)

OCCASIONS

New Year

Choir: 'A New Year Carol' – Benjamin Britten (Boosey & Hawkes)

New Year

- The church calendar begins on Advent Sunday. The idea of inaugurating the new year on 1 January was formally adopted in Scotland in 1600 and in England in 1752. In Scotland the prevailing Presbyterian culture was suspicious of Christmas, so secular Hogmanay traditions grew accordingly.
- Long ago New Year was marked on 25 March – the annunciation of the angel Gabriel to the Virgin Mary – the beginning of the gospel story and a new beginning of all things. When the year started in March, the seventh month was September, the eighth October, and so on. Now we associate New Year with resolutions. You could call them the triumph of hope over experience.

'New every morning is the love'

- This hymn was written by John Keble, a leader of the Oxford Movement, and follows the tradition of infusing every hour of the day, week and year with Christian devotion. It is inspired by the words of Lamentations 2.23 – the steadfast love of the Lord never ceases, God's mercies never come to an end: they are new every morning. Great is God's faithfulness.
- The tune, 'Melcombe', named after a village near Weymouth, is by Samuel Webbe, a cabinetmaker who taught himself six languages and was Roman Catholic.

Hymn: 'New every morning is the love' (Melcombe)

Three anthems

- William Walton was born in Lancashire in 1902. His father was a choirmaster and his mother a singing teacher. He was a chorister and undergraduate at Christ

Church, Oxford. He published concertos and a symphony in the inter-war years and many film scores during World War Two, including the first of Laurence Olivier's major Shakespearean films, *Henry V*. He continued to publish until his death in Italy in 1983. 'What cheer?' is a Christmas carol commissioned by Oxford University Press in 1961 for its collection *Carols for Choirs*. It is set in triple time and sounds like a dance. Walton injects a sense of mischievous play with his use of syncopation.
- Melissa Dunphy was born in 1980 and raised in Australia. She now lives in the USA. 'Halcyon Days', written by her regular collaborator, the poet Jacqueline Goldfinger, portrays a period of calm during winter storms – an opportunity to reflect on what we have lost, but then to arise and face the new year with joy and grace.
- 'The gate of the year' is a line from the poem by Minnie Louise Haskins who taught at the London School of Economics before World War Two. Haskins published a small volume of poetry, *The Desert*, which included the poem 'God Knows', originally written in 1908, to which she added the famous preamble to create the poem that today is commonly known as 'The Gate of the Year'. The words became well known when Queen Elizabeth (the Queen Mother) handed a copy to her husband King George VI which he then quoted in his 1939 Christmas broadcast to the British Empire. The words are engraved on plaques on the gates of the King George VI memorial chapel at Windsor Castle.

Choir: 'What cheer?' – William Walton (Oxford University Press)
Choir: 'Halcyon Days' – Melissa Dunphy (Edition Peters)
Choir: 'The gate of the year' – William Harris (OUP)

'Lord for the years'

- Timothy Dudley-Smith wrote 'Lord for the years' in 1967 for the centenary of the Children's Special Service Mission (founded in 1867), whose functions were taken under the wing of Scripture Union. He originally planned for it to be set to Finlandia, but a tune was written for it by Michael Baughen. It remains his best-known hymn along with 'Tell out my soul'.
- George Carey chose it for his enthronement as Archbishop of Canterbury in 1991. It was much used to mark 50 years after World War Two and at the Millennium.

Hymn: 'Lord for the years' (Lord for the years)

'Auld lang syne'

- 'Auld lang syne' is a Scots poem written by Robert Burns in 1788, set to an old folk song, traditionally sung to bid farewell to the old year at midnight. 'Auld lang syne' means long, long ago or, in this context, old time's sake. At Hogmanay in Scotland, Scots join hands with the person next to them, form a big circle and sing the song together.

Choir: 'Auld lang syne' – arr. Iain Farrington (Novello)

Valentine's Day (14 February)

Choir: *Ubi caritas* – Maurice Duruflé (Durand)

Love

- Love is the seventh virtue, with justice, temperance, prudence, courage, faith and hope. Augustine and Aquinas see love as the crown of the virtues, that contains all the others. It is a central theme for Paul's epistles, but is not even mentioned in Mark's Gospel. English has only one word, but Greek has four: *Storge* means affection and refers to the fondness due to familiarity; *Philia* speaks of friendship, such as that between David and Jonathan in 1 Samuel; *Eros* implies romance, which is in principle an appreciative desire, but can become a god or a prison; finally *Agape* means unconditional regard and is the root of the Christian virtue.
- The most vivid portrayal of love in the Bible is the Song of Songs. Interpreters have hugely diverged on whether this erotic description is the clue to or the opposite of the love of God within the Trinity or between God and humankind.

Valentine

- Nothing is known of St Valentine except that he died in Rome, probably in the third century. Many of the current legends that characterize him were invented in the fourteenth century in England, notably by Geoffrey Chaucer and his circle, when the feast day of 14 February first became associated with romantic love.

'O love that wilt not let me go'

- Written by a Church of Scotland minister after a period of mental suffering, this hymn has powerful imagery of oceans, sun, rainbow and blossom. It is soaked in self-sacrifice: each verse climaxes in the laying down of life, with the last verse offering great reward as a result. It has been described as a hymn of 'ecstatic self-surrender'. The first tune, 'St Margaret', was also written in a Scottish manse, by the then organist of Glasgow Cathedral while staying on Arran.

Hymn: 'O love that wilt not let me go' (Saint Margaret)

Three anthems

- There are three broad ways of thinking about love in Christian tradition. The first is to see it as bad – and to speak of desire, carnal thoughts and the flesh as things to be withstood. The second is uncritical – enjoying the notion of romance, being convinced of 'the one for me', and finding weddings a suitable metaphor for almost everything. The third is truly theological – perceiving all desire as a sublimated desire for God (rather than vice versa).
- 'A new commandment' focuses on Jesus' injunction to his disciples at the Last Supper to love one another. The composer Richard Shephard was based in York as development director at the Minster and wrote widely, but is best known for his church music. He died in 2021.
- 'Upon your heart' was written in 1999, commissioned by Thomas Porter and dedicated to his wife for their 45th wedding anniversary. It is based on Song of Songs 8, and its reference to being sealed upon the lover's heart and arm. The two seals find special resonance with Christ's crucifixion, where his hands are nailed to the cross and his heart is pierced by the spear, thereby sealing us on his heart.
- 'Love bade me welcome' is a poem by George Herbert. The scene is a banquet, to which the poet is invited. But he holds back, afraid of going in. Love continues to invite, asking the poet's reason for withdrawing. The poet says he's not worthy. Love insists the poet is worthy. The poet continues to doubt. Love takes the poet's hand and reels off terms of endearment. The poet continues to draw back. Love continues to turn the tables on the poet. The poet, like the prodigal son, says I will come and serve, but love says no, I will serve you, and the poet finally gives in.

Choir: 'A new commandment' – Richard Shephard (RSCM)
Choir: 'Upon your heart' – Eleanor Daley (OUP)
Choir: 'Love bade me welcome' – Judith Weir (Chester Music)

'Love divine, all loves excelling'

- In 'Love divine, all loves excelling', Charles Wesley offers a prayer for the Saviour to visit the trembling heart, to receive grace enabling the soul to pray and praise, and finally to transform creation into the glory of heaven.
- Wesley wasn't averse to borrowing other poets' work. The last line is adapted from Joseph Addison's hymn: 'When all thy mercies, O my God / My rising soul surveys / Transported with the view, I'm lost / In wonder, love, and praise.' The first line is adapted from John Dryden's verse 'Fairest isle all isles excelling / Seat of pleasure and of loves', from his 1691 poem 'King Arthur'.

Hymn: 'Love divine, all loves excelling' (Blaenwern)

'Goodnight, sweetheart'

- This is a pop song written in 1951 and first sung by the Spaniels in 1953. It's best known for being featured in the 1973 film *American Graffiti* and the 1987 film *Three Men and a Baby*. It highlights a constant theme of love – that of leaving and loss.

Choir: 'Goodnight, sweetheart' – The Spaniels arr. Kirby Shaw (Hal Leonard)

Sea Sunday (July)

Choir: 'Never weather-beaten sail' – Thomas Campion (public domain)

Sea Sunday

- The Genesis conception of creation is threefold. There's the sea of chaos, the cosmic sea, referred to in Revelation and in the famous hymn as the glassy sea, and the earth. Chaos is the abiding characteristic of the sea. The paradox of the ancient world was that travel over land was slow and at risk from robbery. Sea travel was much quicker but liable to shipwreck. The sea as in the Jonah story is always threatening. The crossing of the Red Sea is a sign of God's mastery over chaos, and when Jesus later walks on water and calms the Sea of Galilee, he shows a similar dominance over all that oppresses us. Job speaks of the Leviathan, the monster who rises out of the deep – again something that God finally conquers. Revelation has a sea of fire and a beast from the sea, but eventually in the final vision there is no more sea and chaos is over.

'Eternal Father, strong to save'

- William Whiting was inspired by the dangers of the sea described in Psalm 107 and his own experience of sailing. He wrote his famous hymn 'Eternal Father, strong to save' to encourage a young seaman scared of sailing. The hymn has a long association with the Royal Navy and is sung at Sunday Eucharist at the Old Royal Naval College Chapel in Greenwich. It was sung on 9 August 1941, at a service aboard the Royal Navy battleship HMS *Prince of Wales* attended by Winston Churchill (who requested that the hymn be sung) and Franklin D. Roosevelt at the conference creating the Atlantic Charter. The tune 'Melita' is named after Malta where Paul was shipwrecked.

Hymn: 'Eternal Father, strong to save' (Melita)

Three anthems

- 'They that go down to the sea in ships' is based on Psalm 107.23–31. It perceives the ocean as a place to behold God's presence and glory. Herbert Sumsion (1899–1995) was Organist of Gloucester Cathedral between 1928 and 1967 and Director of Music at Cheltenham Ladies' College between 1928 and 1968. The piece is famous for its rippling organ part with solo melody, resembling a little boat, and for the rising and falling choral writing, representing the waves.
- The text of 'Dear Lord and Father of mankind' is by John Greenleaf Whittier (1807–92), an American Quaker poet. The verses of the hymn are an excerpt from his poem 'The Brewing of Soma' (1872) which was an attack on the 'emotional religion of his time'. The storyline is of Vedic priests brewing and drinking the ritual drink soma in an attempt to experience divinity. It describes the whole population getting drunk on soma. It compares this to some Christians' use of 'music, incense, vigils drear, And trance, to bring the skies more near, Or lift men up to heaven!' But all is in vain, according to Whittier – it is mere intoxication. Whittier ends by describing the true method for contact with the divine, as practised by Quakers: sober lives dedicated to doing God's will, seeking silence and selflessness in order to hear the 'still, small voice' described in 1 Kings 19.11–13 as the authentic voice of God, rather than earthquake, wind or fire. The tune comes from Hubert Parry's oratorio *Judith*.
- 'Crossing the bar' is an 1889 poem by Alfred, Lord Tennyson. It is considered that Tennyson wrote it as an elegy. The poem has a tone of finality and the narrator uses an extended metaphor to compare death with crossing the 'sandbar' between river of life, with its outgoing 'flood', and the ocean that lies beyond [death], the 'boundless deep', to which we return. The Pilot is a metaphor for God, whom the speaker hopes to meet face to face. Tennyson

explained, 'The Pilot has been on board all the while, but in the dark I have not seen him … [He is] that divine and unseen who is always guiding us.'

Choir: 'They that go down to the sea in ships' – Herbert Sumsion (RSCM)
Choir: 'Dear Lord and Father of mankind' – C. H. H. Parry arr. H. A. Chambers (Novello)
Choir: 'Crossing the bar' – Rani Arbo arr. Peter Amidon (Amidon Community Music)

'There's a wideness in God's mercy'

- The Tractarian Frederick Faber wrote this hymn after becoming a Roman Catholic in 1846. His originally Calvinist theology is still discernible in the emphasis the hymn places on God's sovereignty, although now in a much more generous vein. The line 'Though we make his love too narrow with false strictness of our own' tells a whole story of how power has been used in the Church over many centuries.

Hymn: 'There's a wideness in God's mercy' (Corvedale)

'Take me to the water'

- The principal imagery of water in Christianity is around baptism. The theme of baptism played a very significant part on African American spirituals, which often focus on the Ohio River as a crossing-over point (like the Red Sea) from slavery to freedom. Baptism, being entry into becoming the free child of God, was a dangerous practice in the seventeenth-century American South, and consequently forbidden in some states. This spiritual thus points to the water of both earthly and heavenly freedom.

Choir: 'Take me to the water' – Spiritual arr. Rollo Dilworth (Hal Leonard)

Anniversary of the coronation of King Charles III (6 May)

Choir: 'God save the King' – arr. Gordon Jacob (Novello)

King Charles III's coronation

- The fundamental assumption of Charles' coronation was that the king is in continuity with the kings of Israel. The key symbols were imitations of elements of Israelite kingship under Saul, David and Solomon – for example, the singing of 'Zadok the priest'. The implication is that the UK/Britain/England is the new Israel. This all sits uncomfortably with the New Testament, but leapfrogs the earthly Jesus to identify with Christ enthroned on high.
- The Church of England's doctrine is its prayer book. The coronation portrays the unwritten constitution. This is performative authority. The service in Westminster Abbey was royalty set within parliament, supported by the military and blessed by the Church.
- George I was 50th in line to the throne in 1714, but the others were all Catholics and thus ineligible. Previous coronations, including the one in 1953, had fierce anti-Catholic rhetoric. Charles' coronation was set within an Anglican Eucharist. It retained a pledge to uphold Protestantism. But all faiths now processed and greeted, the Moderator of the Church of Scotland gave the Bible, and the Queen in 2012 articulated the role of the Church of England: 'Gently and assuredly, the Church of England has created an environment for other faith communities and indeed people of no faith to live freely' – language echoed in Charles' oath. The king prayed, 'Grant that I may be a blessing to all thy children, of every faith and conviction.' Yet just after Charles declared he was a faithful Protestant, the choir sang an anthem by William Byrd, a Catholic under Elizabeth I, to words by Thomas Cranmer, a Protestant archbishop executed by Mary I.

'Praise, my soul, the King of heaven'

- This hymn was written by H. F. Lyte. It is based on Psalm 103. Like 'Abide with me', another of his hymns, it stresses the reliability and trustworthiness of God: providence is highlighted in the words 'in his hands he gently bears us'. The tune was written by John Goss, organist of St Paul's Cathedral.

Hymn: 'Praise, my soul, the King of heaven' (Praise my soul)

Anniversary of the coronation of King Charles III (6 May)

Three anthems

- 'Coronation Sanctus' by Roxanna Panufnik was commissioned by King Charles III for his coronation. It is a two-minute piece for double choir and organ, described by Roxanna Panufnik as 'festive and glittering'. The music quickly builds and finishes ecstatically, with organ fanfares and flamboyantly colourful harmonies.
- 'Sing for the King' was an open invitation for all choirs to join in song to celebrate the coronation of King Charles III. Joanna Forbes L'Estrange, a British singer, composer and choir director, was commissioned by the Royal School of Church Music to compose a new coronation anthem for this project. 'The mountains shall bring peace', a setting of Psalm 72 and Psalm 149, was performed by choirs throughout the world.
- Andrew Lloyd Webber composed 'Make a joyful noise' for the coronation also. He said the king insisted that the piece, which is based on verses from Psalm 98, should be 'hummable' and joyful, and that it would stand the test of time. 'He wants the anthem sung in churches,' he said. He added that writing the anthem helped him after the death from cancer of his son, Nicholas, six weeks before the coronation, at the age of 43.

Choir: 'Coronation Sanctus' – Roxanna Panufnik (Faber Music)
Choir: 'The mountains shall bring peace' – Joanna Forbes L'Estrange (RSCM)
Choir: 'Make a joyful noise' – Andrew Lloyd Webber (Really Useful Group)

'Christ is made the sure foundation'

- This hymn was translated from the seventh-century Latin by J. M. Neale, a Victorian Anglo-Catholic and doyen of Latin hymn translators. Neale originally set it to plainsong and saw it as a lauds hymn for monastic offices, to be preceded by 'Blessed City heavenly Salem', which was to be sung at the night-vigil. Once it became paired with Henry Purcell's tune 'Westminster Abbey', it became standard for the dedication of a church. The key texts are Ephesians 2, Christ the chief cornerstone and 1 Peter 2 (quoting Isaiah 28), 'behold I lay in Zion a chief cornerstone'.

Hymn: 'Christ is made the sure foundation' (Westminster Abbey)

'I was glad'

- Psalm 122 has been sung at the entrance of every monarch at their coronation since Charles I in 1625. The psalm is a prayer for the peace and prosperity

of Jerusalem, and its use in the coronation service draws a parallel between Jerusalem and the UK, as William Blake did in his poem 'And did those feet in ancient time'. The most famous setting of Psalm 122 is Hubert Parry's 'I was glad', which was first performed at the coronation of Edward VII in 1902. The well-known introduction was added for the coronation of George V in 1911.
- At the first performance of Parry's arrangement at the 1902 coronation, the director of music, Sir Frederick Bridge, misjudged the timing and had finished the anthem before the king had arrived, having to repeat it when the right moment came. Bridge was saved by the organist, Walter Alcock, who improvised in the interim.

Choir: 'I was glad' – C. H. H. Parry (public domain, published by Novello)

World Water Day (22 March)

Choir: *Sicut Cervus* – Palestrina (public domain, published in *European Sacred Music*, OUP)

Water

- In the Bible, water is initially a cosmic force. Thus in creation, the Spirit hovers over the face of the waters, Noah sets his ark afloat on the waters, and Moses guides the children of Israel across the Red Sea. Jonah too encounters the raging sea when he's thrown off the boat to be swallowed by a whale. Jesus engages this sense of cosmic power when he calms the storm on Galilee and when he walks on the water. Mighty rivers meanwhile are a rarity in the Middle East. The promise of still waters in Psalm 23 is about a constant supply of fresh water on which to found life, and when Jesus talks to the Samaritan woman about living water in John 4, it's a wonderfully positive image. Fundamentally the Jordan is the river of transformation: in the Old Testament from wilderness to freedom, as Israel enters the Promised Land in the book of Joshua, and in the Gospels baptism, a similar crossing from death to life.

'Like a mighty river flowing'

- Michael Perry was an evangelical hymnwriter and Vicar of Tonbridge who died tragically young in his forties. Unusually for an evangelical hymn, 'Like a mighty river flowing' focuses not on how Jesus gives us peace, but on what that peace feels like. In each verse there are two analogies from creation followed by a turn

to human experience of friendship or forgiveness. The whole hymn dwells on Paul's memorable phrase about the peace of God that passes all understanding.
- The tune, composed by Noël Tredinnick, doyen of All Souls Langham Place music-making, is named 'Old Yeavering' after the birthplace of Christianity in north Northumberland, where Paulinus first baptized converts to Christianity in the seventh century.

Hymn: 'Like a mighty river flowing' (Old Yeavering)

Three anthems

- The baptism of Jesus at the Jordan by John the Baptist appears in all four Gospels, although we tend to think of it in the way it's presented in Matthew and Luke, where three things happen: the heavens open, the Spirit descends as a dove, and a voice speaks, saying, 'You are my beloved son, my favour rests on you.' One interpreter speaks of the way this means to those being baptized, heaven is open to you, God's Spirit is in you, you mean everything to God. The Jordan is the place where Israel entered the promised land under Joshua, but crossing the water also holds resonances of crossing the Red Sea under Moses 40 years before, so there's a sense of freedom from slavery as well as freedom to dwell in a land of their own. Here's the setting of Psalm 42 by Judith Weir, written for the funeral of Queen Elizabeth II in 2022.
- James Whitbourn's 'Pure river of water of life' refers to the portrayal in the book of Revelation of a heaven in which there are no tears and there is no night. It echoes the tree of Genesis 3 from which the forbidden fruit came, by speaking of the tree whose leaves are for the healing of the nations.
- In his 'Rivers of living water', Trevor Weston weaves together Psalm 105 and John 7 to portray the lively rivers, in contrast to the parched land. The long and interweaving vocal lines and the alternation of organ and unaccompanied participation all contribute to the verdant and fertile tone.

Choir: 'Like as the hart' – Judith Weir (Novello)
Choir: 'Pure river of water of life' – James Whitbourn (Chester Music)
Choir: 'Rivers of living water' – Trevor Weston (OUP)

'I heard the voice of Jesus say'

- The Great Disruption was a schism in 1843 in which 450 evangelical ministers broke away from the 1,200-strong clergy of the Church of Scotland to form the Free Church of Scotland. The main conflict was over whether the Church of Scotland or the British government had the power to control clerical positions and benefits. Reunion didn't take place till 1929, and has only been partial.

- Horatio Bonar wrote this hymn shortly before he joined the Free Church schism. Each verse has a specific Gospel text – Matthew 11, John 4, John 8.
- The tune 'Kingsfold' was written by Ralph Vaughan Williams for the original *English Hymnal* in 1906.

Hymn: 'I heard the voice of Jesus say' (Kingsfold)

'Like a mighty stream'

- 'Lift every voice and sing' is often known as the African American national anthem. Here Moses Hogan conflates it with words taken from Amos 5. Amos constantly denounces those who make gestures of piety but don't back them up with justice and fairness. They continue with harsh taxes, bribes and oppression. The Revd Dr Martin Luther King Jr quoted Amos 5.24 in his 1963 Letter from a Birmingham Jail, criticizing white clergy in these terms: 'We know through painful experience that freedom is never voluntarily given by the oppressor; it must be demanded by the oppressed. Frankly, I have yet to engage in a direct-action campaign that was "well timed" in the view of those who have not suffered unduly from the disease of segregation. For years now I have heard the word "Wait!" It rings in the ear of every Negro with piercing familiarity. This "Wait" has almost always meant "Never." We must come to see, with one of our distinguished jurists, that "justice too long delayed is justice denied."'

Choir: 'Like a mighty stream' – Moses Hogan and John Jacobson (Hal Leonard)

International Day of Peace (21 September)

Choir: 'I will be a child of peace' – Elaine Hagenberg (Beckenhorst Press)

International Day of Peace

- This day was first marked in 1982. United Nations Secretary-General António Guterres directed the world's attention to this event in these words: 'Peace is needed today more than ever. War and conflict are unleashing devastation, poverty, and hunger, and driving tens of millions of people from their homes. Climate chaos is all around. And even peaceful countries are gripped by gaping inequalities and political polarisation.' He also carefully connects the theme of peace to the Sustainable Development Goals created in 2015.

International Day of Peace (21 September)

- One author says this about peace: 'Peace is not a past state to which we expect, and feel entitled, to return, but is instead an aspiration towards which we invite God to lead us and at which we never expect fully to arrive. Peace is a process, not an original starting-point or a foreseeable destination. It's about relationships. Relationships are not like buildings, which are opened when all is working well and begin to decay from that moment on. They're more like gardens, which begin from the dust, and gradually take root and flourish, and yet need pruning and attention and are never in a place of static perfection or repose. Sometimes toward the end of a conflict people refer to the "peace process"; but in truth the phrase is a tautology, because peace is always a process.'

'Lord, make us servants of your peace'

- The Prayer of St Francis of Assisi, sometimes known as the Peace Prayer, wasn't written by St Francis in the twelfth century. It was written in 1912 by a French Catholic priest, Esther Bouquerel, and published in a small-circulation spiritual magazine. At the end of World War One, the French Franciscan Étienne Benoît printed millions of copies of the prayer on a card that depicted St Francis on the back. A few years later an English translation was printed in a Quaker magazine in the USA under the title 'A Prayer of St Francis of Assisi' – and the rest is history.
- 'Lord, make us servants of your peace' was written by Fr James Quinn SJ (1919–2010), a Scottish Jesuit who grew up in Glasgow. He saw hymnwriting as a kind of preaching. His hymns are scriptural, doctrinal and eucharistic.

Hymn: 'Lord, make us servants of your peace' (O Waly Waly)

Three anthems

- 'We shall walk through the valley in peace' is an African American spiritual, rooted in Psalm 23.4, 'Yea, though I walk through the valley of the shadow of death, I will fear no evil: for thou art with me.' The 'valley' is a poignant theme in African American songs, including, 'Jesus walked this lonesome valley' and 'Down to the river to pray'. It refers to resilience and endurance.
- Amy Beach was America's first successful female composer, coming to prominence in the 1880s and continuing her career till she died in 1944. She bases this peace on Jesus' words in John 14.27, 'Peace I leave with you; my peace I give to you. I do not give to you as the world gives. Do not let your hearts be troubled, and do not let them be afraid.' There is always a tension between whether Jesus is referring to an inner peace or an outer, public one – and a question about which is the more important.

- *The Armed Man* is a Requiem Mass by Welsh composer Karl Jenkins, subtitled 'A Mass for Peace'. It was commissioned by the Royal Armouries Museum to mark its move from London to Leeds, and was dedicated to victims of the war in Kosovo. It charts with growing menace the descent into war, interspersed with moments of reflection; it demonstrates the horrors that war brings; and it concludes with the hope for peace in a new millennium, when 'sorrow, pain and death can be overcome'. *The Armed Man* stands in the tradition of Benjamin Britten's *War Requiem* as the commemoration of war through pointing a path to peace.

Choir: 'We shall walk through the valley in peace' – arr. Undine Smith Moore (Augsburg)
Choir: 'Peace I leave with you' – Amy Beach (public domain)
Choir: 'Benedictus' from *The Armed Man: A Mass for Peace* (Boosey & Hawkes)

'Peace, perfect peace'

- Arguments about whether peace without justice is really peace, either practically or conceptually, and arguments about whether peace is a goal or a process, will always continue. The principle of this simple chorus is that however hard we may work for peace – and some may fight for peace – peace is, in the end, a gift.
- As the same author says, 'It's not that we know what resurrection looks like and peace is a helpful analogy of that resurrection. The resurrection of Jesus – in its immediate sense of the body raised after crucifixion, and in its wider sense of the forgiveness, resurrection and healing that are recorded in the post-resurrection Gospel accounts – is precisely an account of what peace entails. Peace is, in the end, resurrection.' And resurrection is an unequivocal gift.

Hymn: 'Peace, perfect peace' (Peace, perfect peace)

'I've got peace like a river'

- This spiritual compares the peace of God to a flowing river, the joy of Christ to a bubbling fountain, and the love of God to a wide ocean. All three have multiple layers of significance. They appear among the first three fruits of the Spirit in Galatians 5; but furthermore every river in spirituals has some connection to the Ohio river, which formed the boundary between slavery and freedom, and every ocean has some link to the Atlantic, across which Africans were for centuries brought from freedom to slavery. Martin Luther King famously quoted Amos' description of peace flowing like a mighty river and justice like a never-failing stream.

Choir: 'I've got peace like a river' – arr. Mary McDonald (Lorenz Corporation)

World Space Week (4–10 October)

Choir: 'A Cosmic Prayer' – Carson Cooman (Wayne Leupold Editions)

Space

- Of all the tensions between today and the ancient world view, the notion that heaven is above the sky is the greatest. It speaks to the assumption of a flat earth, and what one twentieth-century theologian called the three-decker universe – heaven, earth and hell. It assumes an idea that God dwells above us, where angels fly and surround the throne of grace. The French word for heaven is *ciel*. Many scriptural stories assume such a configuration – the ladder of Jacob and the angels, Elijah's chariot, and Jesus' Ascension among them.
- In the Bible, above is both remote and superior. Heaven is often mentioned as a throne, and in John 14 as a house with rooms; in other places as a temple, a city or decorated with jewels.
- The major question is of where God is post-sky. Theologically this is resolved by Christ's incarnation: God is with us. But still the question of post-mortem life and the whole idea of another realm abides. One way to think of this is to imagine essence, that which lasts for ever, as one side of an hourglass and existence, that which lasts for a limited time, as the other side – and the aperture between them being Jesus.

'Lord of the boundless curves of space'

- This hymn was written by Albert Bayly, a twentieth-century Congregationalist minister who also wrote librettos for William Lloyd Webber cantatas. He was particularly committed to providing hymns that spoke to the reality of the universe as now understood – he also wrote 'O Lord of every shining constellation'. For Bayly, there is an achievement that goes beyond God's work in creation: and that is of his recreation of humankind in Christ.

Hymn: 'Lord of the boundless curves of space' (San Rocco)

Three anthems

- With characteristic elegant simplicity, Lucy Walker takes the opening words of Henry Vaughan's 'The World' and delicately evokes Vaughan's understated reverie, in his words, 'I saw eternity the other night / Like a great ring of pure and endless light.'

- Ola Gjeilo is a contemporary Norwegian-American composer. The words for this piece come from the Song of Songs. The northern lights, or aurora borealis, are dancing waves of light. Energized particles from the sun thud into Earth's upper atmosphere at speeds of up to 45 million mph, but our planet's magnetic field protects us from them. As Earth's magnetic field redirects the particles towards the poles the dramatic process transforms into a cinematic atmospheric phenomenon.
- 'Seek him that maketh the seven stars' is a setting of Psalm 139. The anthem begins with an image of the night sky. The organ's high registers evoke the twinkling stars. The repeated 'Seek him' starts in devotional longing but eventually becomes a joyful dance, finally resolving into restful serenity. 'Seek him' was commissioned by the Royal Academy of Arts, and first performed at St James' Piccadilly in May 1995.

Choir: 'I saw eternity' – Lucy Walker (Lucy Walker)
Choir: 'Northern Lights' – Ola Gjeilo (Walton Music)
Choir: 'Seek him that maketh the seven stars' – Dove (Faber Music)

'The spacious firmament on high'

- Joseph Addison published an article in *The Spectator* in 1712 commending practices for strengthening faith – particularly harmonizing scriptural faith with Newtonian physics – which had emerged in 1704 and 1707. Addison argued, 'The Supreme Being has made the best arguments for his own existence, in the formation of the heavens and the earth, and these are arguments which a man of sense cannot forbear attending to, who is out of the noise and hurry of human affairs.' Then he offered this poem. The hymn sums up the confidence that Newtonian maths and physics simply underwrote the Christian faith.

Hymn: 'The spacious firmament on high' (Addison's)

'Fly me to the moon'

- This song was written in 1954 and covered in 1964 by Frank Sinatra. It was closely associated with NASA's Apollo space programme. It became the first music heard on the moon when it was played on a portable cassette player by Apollo 11 astronaut Buzz Aldrin after he stepped onto the moon in 1969.

Choir: 'Fly me to the moon' – Bart Howard arr. Kirby Shaw (Hal Leonard)

CHORAL WORKS

Allegri's Miserere

Choir: 'Cast me not away' – Samuel Sebastian Wesley (public domain, published by Novello)

Allegri and the Miserere

- Gregorio Allegri was a priest who was appointed to the cathedral in Fermo, on the Adriatic coast, 150 miles north-east of Rome. His motets brought him to the attention of Pope Urban and an appointment to sing as a contralto in the choir of the Sistine Chapel in Rome in 1629–52. He is credited with creating the first string quartet.
- The Miserere is a setting of Psalm 51 for use in the Sistine Chapel during the Tenebrae service on Wednesday and Good Friday of Holy Week. The service began at dusk (*tenebrae* is Latin for 'shadows' or 'darkness'). Seven candles were extinguished one by one, save for the last candle, which remained alight and was then hidden. Allegri envisioned the setting of the Miserere to be the final act within the first lesson of the Tenebrae service. The question of what to do with the last candle is profoundly theological – extinguishing it seems painful, terrifying or devastating. It could remain lit, be hidden, be extinguished, or be relit. Each approach has a whole theology of the cross behind it.

Mystery

- It became forbidden to transcribe the music for the Miserere, and it was allowed to be performed only at those particular services at the Sistine Chapel. The story goes that the 14-year-old Wolfgang Amadeus Mozart was visiting Rome when he first heard the piece during the Wednesday service. Later that day, he wrote it down entirely from memory, returning to the Chapel that Friday to make minor corrections. Less than three months after hearing the song and transcribing it, Mozart had gained fame for the work. He was summoned to Rome by Pope Clement XIV, who showered praise on him for his feat of musical genius and awarded him the Chivalric Order of the Golden Spur. The British historian

Charles Burney obtained the piece from Mozart and took it to London, where it was published in 1771. It was also transcribed by Felix Mendelssohn and Franz Liszt. Since the lifting of the ban, Allegri's Miserere has become one of the most popular a cappella choral works now performed.

'Lord Jesus, think on me'

- This hymn was written by a fifth-century contemporary and friend of Augustine of Hippo, who was a soldier, philosopher and poet, and became Bishop of Cyrene in modern Libya in 410. He was fond of paradoxes and sometimes struggled with propositional ways of expressing Christian doctrine. This hymn is the last of ten odes in which he described the mystery of God: here he adopts the persona of the 'good thief' crucified with Jesus and asks the Saviour to remember him. It was translated in 1876 by Allen Chatfield, who resurrected many early Greek Christian texts. The tune was published in 1579 by William Daman, who probably came originally from Italy.

Hymn: 'Lord Jesus, think on me' (Southwell)

Psalm 51 and David

- David is associated with the zenith of Israel's power, prestige and closeness to God. He is the figure Israel always looks back to – the author of the psalms, the one who reigned when the kingdom was at its largest extent. Yet his story is one of transformation from a shepherd boy with five smooth stones to a bloated monarch with no inhibitions. After his son Solomon's reign, Israel devolved into two kingdoms then each went into exile.
- 2 Samuel 11 tells of a time when David should have been at war; but he espied Bathsheba naked, desired her, and made her pregnant. He tried to pass off the child as Uriah's, but Uriah wouldn't go in to his wife Bathsheba, so David put him in the heat of battle and he was killed. The prophet Nathan then tells the story of a rich man who took away a poor man's only ewe lamb. David grows angry. Then Nathan says, 'You are the man!' David is penitent. The baby dies; but later Bathsheba gives birth to Solomon.
- Psalm 51 turns this story into a prayer. It is made up of 19 verses in six parts with a hinge at verse 10, 'Create in me a clean heart.' Verses 1–2 are an appeal for cleansing, 3–6 acknowledge the nature of the wrongdoing, 7–9 offer a further appeal for cleansing, 10–12 seek inner renewal, 13–15 testify to God's deliverance, and 16–19 conclude with a plea for the restoration of the city. Sin is rebellion, failure, waywardness and evil. Cleansing is liturgical: the psalm speaks of wiping away, washing and purifying. There are three kinds of inner transform-

ation: a clean heart, presence and the joy of deliverance. The result is a renewed mission to speak of God's mercies; and the context is always political – after all, David's failure was to use his royal power in the service of his own desires rather than the needs of the kingdom.
- Here are three treatments of Psalm 51, finishing with Allegri's.

Choir: *Miserere mei* – William Byrd (public domain, published in *The Oxford Book of Tudor Anthems*, OUP)
Choir: 'Turn thy face from my sins' – Thomas Attwood (public domain, published by RSCM)
Choir: *Miserere mei, Deus* – Gregorio Allegri (public domain, published in *European Sacred Music*, Oxford University Press)

'Just as I am, without one plea'

- Charlotte Elliot lived with her brother Henry, a vicar in Brighton. She was too sick to assist with a bazaar to raise money for the daughters of poor clergy, so she stayed home and wrote this hymn. Her brother ruefully reflected that this single hymn saw more gospel fruit than the whole of his ministry. It was published in the *Invalid's Hymnbook* in 1836, with the verse 'Him that cometh unto me I will in no wise cast out' (John 6.37). It is distinctive in making reference to healing the mind as part of what Christianity offers. The tune 'Saffron Walden', written by Arthur Henry Brown, who spent almost all his life in Essex and named the tune after a famous Essex town, turns the final line of each stanza into a humble prayer.

Hymn: 'Just as I am, without one plea' (Saffron Walden)

'Wash me throughly'

- Samuel Sebastian Wesley was the eldest child of his father Samuel's second family, and the grandson of Charles Wesley. His middle name was a tribute to Johann Sebastian Bach. He was organist at several cathedrals before becoming a professor at the Royal Academy of Music in 1850. He is best known for his short anthem 'Lead me, Lord', which is an excerpt from a longer 1861 piece, 'Praise the Lord, O my soul'. Here is his 1840 setting of Psalm 51.

Choir: 'Wash me throughly' – Samuel Sebastian Wesley

Vivaldi's Gloria

Choir: *Gloria in excelsis Deo* (from *Gloria*) – Antonio Vivaldi

Vivaldi

- Vivaldi lived from 1678 to 1741. He was a Catholic priest and violinist as well as a composer, and spent most of his life in Venice. When he wrote his Magnificat he was working as choir master at an institution known as Pietà. This was a charitable home for foundlings. The orphanage had a fascinating and brilliant business model. It literally trained its orphans to sing for their supper. Vivaldi's job was to compose pieces of music and rehearse his choir of young orphans to sing them, so as to attract to chapel services a wealthy congregation who would, through their donations and bequests, support and finance the institution. Catholic Europe did not countenance mixed church choirs in the early eighteenth century. The boys would leave the orphanage and enter apprenticeships. It was left to the girls to make up the choir. If you look at the score of Vivaldi's Magnificat, you'll see that the vocal bass parts are pitched high enough that they can be sung by the all-female choir of the Pietà.
- If you look from the score of the music to the words of the canticle, you realize the significance of what Vivaldi was doing. Lowly young girls, with no hopes, prospects or protectors, were taken up, given a song to sing, and offered a chance to bring about their own redemption and the liberation of others like them. They were truly singing Mary's song. Through them the Holy Spirit was exalting the humble and meek, and sending the rich away a good deal emptier. They were incubating the gospel of transformation, just as Mary in her womb was incubating the word of God.

'Glory be to God the Father'

- Horatius Bonar was a Scottish minister and hymnwriter who moved to the Free Church after the 1843 Disruption and became Moderator of its General Assembly. He wrote this hymn for an English Presbyterian Church hymn book. It is based on the fourth-century 'conclusion', Gloria Patri, known as the 'Lesser Doxology', sung at the end of psalms and canticles. Bonar wrote 600 hymns, including many for children who did not enjoy singing psalms. Regent Square was composed for this hymn by Henry Smart, and is called after a Presbyterian church in London.

Hymn: 'Glory be to God the Father' (Regent Square)

Gloria

- The Gloria is a second- or third-century Greek hymn roughly contemporaneous with the Te Deum and Hail Gladdening Light. There were many such hymns, but most have been dismissed as heretical. It was translated into Latin around 350 by Hilary of Poitiers, who spent a period of exile in the East. It must have been translated before Jerome's Latin translation of the Scriptures (the Vulgate, 385), because it uses the word '*excelsis*' for 'the highest', rather than Jerome's '*altissimis*'. The Latin version is a good deal shorter than the original Greek. It is clearly trinitarian, with a clear articulation of Jesus' role as our advocate at the right hand of the Father, but with a brief mention of the Holy Spirit.
- In the Roman Mass, largely adopted in shape by mainstream Protestant churches in liturgical reforms of the 1960s, the Gloria comes straight after the kyrie (the confession of sin and absolution) as a celebration of forgiveness and eternal life. It is omitted during Advent and Lent. In the 1662 Book of Common Prayer it comes after communion because the prayer book locates confession as a response to the word and the Gloria as a response to the whole act of joining the angels in communion.
- The Gloria makes angels' song one for the whole Church. We all join with the angels as did the shepherds in Luke 2. By the birth of Jesus, the division between sinful humans and glorious angels is ended and all sing God's glory together.
- The major difference lies between 'peace to his people on earth' and 'peace to all people of good will'. This distinction lies on the question of whether it's necessary to recognize God's glory to receive its benefits. Vivaldi is not portraying a peace that has already been achieved, but a peace that is desperately sought amid the troubles of the world. The harrowing and emotional content of his peace section, with several key changes, is his answer.

Choir: *Et in terra pax*
Choir: *Gratias agimus tibi – Propter magnam gloriam*
Choir: *Domine, Fili unigenite*
Choir: *Domine Deus, Agnus Dei*

'All glory be to God on high'

- This is Timothy Dudley-Smith's arrangement of the Gloria, sung to the tune John Ireland wrote for 'Dear Lord and Father of Mankind'. Timothy Dudley-Smith was Bishop of Thetford. He wrote in these terms about the effect of his father's death while he was still a child: 'I vividly remember my poor mother taking me quietly aside and telling me he was not going to get better. Of course I prayed; and you would imagine that on his death I would have abandoned my childish praying as useless. I can only think that, without my earthly father, I felt more keenly the need for a heavenly one.'

Hymn: 'All glory be to God on high' (Repton)

Glory

- The purpose of all things, as for example stated in the Westminster Shorter Catechism, is that we are in right relationship to God – our goal is to glorify and enjoy God for ever. The key verse in articulating this is John 1.14 – 'and we have beheld his glory'. The Old Testament focused on the Temple – the ark, the fire, and most of all the *shekinah*, the brightness of God's appearance. A vital question is whether God is present in the same way in the second Temple as in the first – given that several of these key features are missing. When Jesus appears, he constitutes the answer to the sense of lack that had lingered since the loss of the ark in the destruction of the first Temple.
- Glory is ultimately about experiencing in human relations the quality of the divine relations within the Trinity. It's about relationship. Singing is an important part of discovery.

Choir: *Quoniam – Cum Sancto Spiritu*

Handel's *The Messiah*

Choir: 'And the glory, the glory of the Lord' (from *The Messiah*) – George Frideric Handel

The Messiah

- Handel's 1741 oratorio *The Messiah* comes in three parts. The oratorio follows the liturgical year: Part I covers Advent, Christmas and the life of Jesus; Part II covers Lent, Easter, Ascension and Pentecost; Part III covers the end of the church year, dealing with the end of time, the resurrection of the dead and Christ's glorification in heaven.
- The words are drawn mostly from the Old Testament: thus the birth and death of Jesus are told in the words of the prophet Isaiah. There is almost nothing on Jesus' ministry – the only such aria is 'He shall feed His flock like a shepherd' – on account of the reluctance to portray Jesus on stage, perhaps caused by the

laws against blasphemy that persisted until recent decades. Unlike Handel's other oratorios, there is no narrative and no dialogue.
- The theology is postlapsarian: while there is no account of Creation or Fall, the oratorio portrays the coming of Christ as an idea formulated during the time of the prophets. If one thinks of the scriptural drama as a five-act play – Creation, Israel, Jesus, Church, Eschaton – the Hallelujah Chorus comes at the juncture between Act 4 and Act 5 – celebrating either the ultimate success of the Church or the moment when God takes over, things being as bad as could be.

'Rejoice, the Lord is king'

- The librettist for *The Messiah* was Charles Jennens; he lived at Gopsall Hall in Leicestershire, where *The Messiah* was composed. In 1826, Charles Wesley's son Samuel found three hymn tunes by Handel in the Fitzwilliam Museum in Cambridge, and named one of them 'Gopsal'.
- Charles Wesley was inspired to write this hymn by Ephesians 1.19–22, which speaks of how the Father set Christ in the heavenly places and put all things under his feet. This is echoed in the Apostles' Creed in the words 'He sits at the right hand of the Father'. There are also clear references to Philippians 4.4 and Psalm 97. The refrain is taken from the response at the beginning of the Eucharistic Prayer: 'lift up your hearts'. The climax comes from 1 Corinthians 15. One commentator calls this 'the greatest of all triumph hymns', not least for the concatenation of scriptural images.

Hymn: 'Rejoice, the Lord is king' (Gopsal)

Origins of the term 'Hallelujah'

- The term 'Hallelujah' is made up of two elements: the second-person imperative plural *hallelu* – 'praise!' and *Yah* – the Lord. Thus it is often translated 'Praise the Lord'. It is a request for a congregation to join in praise towards God. The term is found 24 times in the Psalms and four times in Revelation. By the third century BCE, Jews had ceased using the name Yahweh, and often substituted Adonai (the Lord). Christians often do the same – thus the LORD is found in capitals in many translations of the Old Testament.
- Revelation 19, the great song of praise to God for triumph over the Whore of Babylon, is the key source for Charles Jennens' construction of the Hallelujah Chorus. The Greek version, 'Alleluia', is associated with the Easter season and avoided in Lent.
- 'Yahweh' is articulated in the burning bush story (Exodus 3.14) as God's name – I am who I am – a name whose significance is amplified in Jesus' 'I am'

sayings in John's Gospel. In 1878, Julius Wellhausen advanced the documentary hypothesis, which suggested the Pentateuch was derived from four sources, one of which (the Yahwist) was distinctive because it called God Yahweh and saw God as anthropomorphic in body and mind. The word 'Israel' is based on the Canaanite name 'El' rather than Yahweh. The centre of Yahwist worship lay in three great annual festivals coinciding with major events in rural life: Passover with the birthing of lambs, Shavuot with the cereal harvest, and Sukkot with the fruit harvest. These became linked to events in the national consciousness of Israel: Passover with the exodus from Egypt, Shavuot with the law-giving at Sinai, and Sukkot with the wilderness wanderings. The festivals thus celebrated Yahweh's salvation of Israel and Israel's status as his holy people.
- Here are four anthems from the different parts of *The Messiah*.

Choir: 'For unto us a child is born'
Choir: 'Behold the Lamb of God'
Choir: 'Lift up your heads, O ye gates'
Choir: 'Since by man came death'

'Thine be the glory'

- The tune for 'Thine be the glory' was originally written as part of Handel's oratorio *Joshua*, but he transferred it to *Judas Maccabaeus*, where it became the chorus 'See the conquering hero comes'.
- The text is a free translation of the work of the early twentieth-century Swiss hymnwriter Edmund Budry. The repeated 'victory' can be traced to St Paul in 1 Corinthians 15.57: 'But thanks be to God who giveth us the victory through our Lord Jesus Christ'. The translation was made by Richard Hoyle, a Baptist minister and gifted linguist who translated hymns from a dozen languages.

Hymn: 'Thine be the glory' (Maccabaeus)

Hallelujah Chorus

- The well-known Hallelujah Chorus is the closing piece of the second part of *The Messiah*. Entirely drawn from Revelation, it comes in four main sections. It starts with 'for the Lord God omnipotent reigneth', woven together by hallelujahs; it then moves into 'The kingdom of this world is become', a four-part setting like a chorale; it approaches its climax with 'And he shall reign for ever and ever', which resembles Philipp Nicolai's Lutheran chorale '*Wachet auf*', known in English as 'Sleepers wake'; then finally, like a wave breaking above another wave on the seashore, comes 'King of Kings … and Lord of Lords', sung on one note, energized by repeated calls of 'Hallelujah' and 'for ever – and ever', raised higher and higher, up to a final solemn 'Hallelujah'. The overall effect is of basking in the glory of God.

Choir: 'Hallelujah Chorus'

Mozart's Requiem

Choir: *Introitus: Requiem aeternam* (from *Requiem*) – Wolfgang Amadeus Mozart

Mozart

- Mozart composed part of the Requiem in Vienna in late 1791. He left it unfinished at his death on 5 December the same year. A completed version, dated 1792, by Franz Süssmayr was delivered to Count Franz von Walsegg, who commissioned the piece for a Requiem service to commemorate the anniversary of his wife's death. Mozart received only half of the payment in advance, so upon his death his widow Constanze was keen to have the work completed secretly by someone else, submit it to the count as having been completed by Mozart and collect the final payment. There have been countless other completions, including many modern ones.
- There are several myths about the Requiem. One is that Mozart received the commission from a mysterious messenger who did not reveal the commissioner's identity. It is said Mozart came to believe that he was writing the Requiem for his own funeral and that he had been poisoned. Peter Schaffer's play *Amadeus* is based on an earlier Pushkin play and a Rimsky-Korsakov opera.
- The Requiem was played at the funerals of Haydn, Beethoven, Schubert, Goethe, Napoleon, Chopin and Berlioz.

'In heavenly love abiding'

- Anna Laetitia Warning wrote this reflection on trust in 1850. It is full of scriptural references – the stilling of the storm in Mark 4, the work of the shepherd in Psalm 23, abiding in Christ's love in John 15, and delivery from fear in Psalm 34. The tune was written by David Jenkins, Professor of Music in Aberystwyth, for the wedding of the local MP in 1898.

Hymn: 'In heavenly love abiding' (Penlan)

Requiem

- A requiem is a Roman Catholic Mass offered for the repose of the soul of one or more deceased persons. It is usually celebrated in the context of a funeral. Musical settings of the propers of the Requiem Mass are also called Requiems, and the term has subsequently been applied to other musical compositions associated with death, dying and mourning, even when they lack religious or liturgical relevance. The name comes from the introit of the liturgy, which begins '*Requiem aeternam dona eis, Domine*' – 'Grant them eternal rest, O Lord'.
- Unlike a conventional Mass, there is no prayer before the Gospel procession, no incense, Alleluia or acolytes at the Gospel, no sharing of the peace, no Gloria or Creed, and the dismissal is replaced by *Requiescant in pace*. Vestments are traditionally black although purple or white are often worn today. The sequence '*Dies irae*', recited or sung before the Gospel, is an obligatory part of the Requiem Mass in the earlier forms. As its opening words '*Dies irae*' ('day of wrath') indicate, it speaks of the Day of Judgement in fearsome terms; it then appeals to Jesus for mercy.
- Since Vatican II, the Requiem has gained a more positive emphasis. It is now known as the Mass of the Resurrection. But it remains rooted in the notion of purgatory, and the necessity of praying for the departed so they may more swiftly reach paradise.
- The following pieces all come from Mozart's Requiem. The Rex tremendae is a celebration of the majesty of God. The Lacrimosa is a lament for this tearful day. The Sanctus, as in most Eucharistic celebrations, comes in the Eucharistic Prayer between the preface and the words of institution or anamnesis.

Choir: *Rex tremendae*
Choir: *Lacrimosa*
Choir: *Sanctus*

'Rock of ages, cleft for me'

- This hymn was written in 1763 by Augustus Toplady. The story goes that Toplady drew his inspiration from an incident in the gorge of Burrington Combe in the Mendip Hills in England. Toplady, a preacher in the nearby village of Blagdon, was travelling along the gorge when he was caught in a storm. Finding shelter in a gap in the gorge, he was struck by the title and scribbled down the initial lyrics.
- Toplady was a Calvinist opponent of John Wesley. His father died in 1741 during the War of Jenkins' Ear, part of the War of the Austrian Succession, when Augustus was a few months old. Toplady published a 700-page argument that the Church of England had always been committed to Calvinist tenets such as

predestination. He was the first to identify the five points of Calvinism – total depravity, unconditional election, limited atonement, irresistible grace and the perseverance of the saints (sometimes given the acronym 'tulip'). John Wesley thought of the 'double cure' in this hymn as justification by Christ and sanctification by the Holy Spirit.

Hymn: Rock of ages, cleft for me (Petra)

Cum sanctis tuis

- This is the very last section of the Requiem, which largely repeats the opening.

Choir: *Cum sanctis tuis*

Haydn's *The Creation*

Choir: In the beginning (from *The Creation*) – Franz Josef Haydn

Creation and Haydn

- Haydn wrote in 1802 that 'Often, when I was struggling with all kinds of obstacles ... a secret voice whispered to me: "There are so few happy and contented people in this world; sorrow and grief follow them everywhere; perhaps your labour will become a source from which the careworn ... will for a while derive peace and refreshment."' The first public performance of *The Creation* was in Vienna on 19 March 1799. The work became a favourite of the Tonkünstler-societät, a charitable organization for the support of widows and orphans of musicians, for which Haydn frequently performed, often with huge ensembles, for the rest of his career. The London premiere, using the English text, came in 1800, at Covent Garden.
- The three sources on which the oratorio draws are Genesis, the Psalms and John Milton's *Paradise Lost*. The oratorio is structured in three parts. The first deals with the creation of light, of heaven and earth, of the sun and moon, of the land and water, and of plants (Days 1–4). The second treats the creation of the animals, and of man and woman (5–6). The final part describes Adam and Eve during their happy time in the Garden of Eden, portraying an idealized love in harmony with the 'new world' (7). With its picture of a benign, rationally ordered universe and its very positive view of humanity (the Fall is referred to

only casually just before the final chorus), *The Creation* fitted the mood of the Enlightenment, both in Georgian England and in 1790s Vienna.
- Its theological content, minimizing conflict, guilt and retribution, also chimed in with Haydn's own personal faith – 'Not of the gloomy, always suffering sort, but rather cheerful and reconciled', as an early biographer put it. Indeed, in composing the oratorio he felt he was performing an act of religious devotion. However, the Roman Catholic Church took offence at its non-moralistic tone and alleged secularity, and banned it from places of worship. As the century progressed, the work's reputation fell steadily elsewhere. In England *The Creation* often suffered from adverse comparisons with the widely celebrated Handel. Attacks on the work became routine, with Hector Berlioz outdoing all comers in vitriol: 'I have always felt a profound antipathy for this work ... its lowing oxen, its buzzing insects, its light in C, which dazzles like a Carcel lamp; and then its Adam, Uriel, Gabriel, and the flute solos and all the amiabilities really shrivel me up – they make me want to murder someone.'

'Praise to the Lord'

- This hymn was originally written in German in 1680 to go with a folk tune, today known as '*Lobe den Herren*'. It became famous and was known to be Kaiser Frederick William III's favourite after he heard it sung on a visit to the mines in 1800. What's really fascinating is that whereas salvation in 1680 was seen in terms of angels playing harps on clouds, by the Victorian era it meant health and social progress. One critic described Catherine Winkworth's translation of this hymn as an example of 'muscular Christianity tinged with philistinism'. The same critic accuses Winkworth of importing 'a nineteenth-century flavour of feminine resignation'.
- It's certainly a vigorous, unselfconscious proclamation of Christian conviction. Notice how in each of the three verses, we start by addressing our own soul with news of God's glory, and then turn to one another to pay heed to what God has done.

Hymn: 'Praise to the Lord' (Lobe den Herren)

Creation and God

- Creation is neither an arbitrary accidental appearance nor a quixotic display of divine power, nor a primal battle between good and evil. It is the beginning of a covenant. God provides abundance and wonder. We respond with praise, gratitude and obedience.

- There are two scriptural creation stories. Genesis 1 is a majestic liturgical poem, with its refrain, 'It is good. It is very good.' It describes order amid chaos, it speaks of trustworthy food production, it portrays humanity as priest of creation, and the sabbath as the crown of creation: God didn't rest because God was tired. Meanwhile Genesis 2 is focused on the place of humanity. Humankind is part of the earth – made from its dust – and is charged with being caretaker for the rest. Humanity has limits: it *is not God*, but more like the rest of creation. Together these two accounts describe creation as grand and abundant but precarious and vulnerable.
- Other scriptural texts embellish aspects of creation. Five psalms voice Israel's confidence in and gratitude for God's plentiful world. Isaiah 40—55 arises from exile, and portrays Israel's God as stronger than the Babylonian gods. Isaiah 65 offers a picture of the new creation, and furnishes what became the book of Revelation. Matthew echoes all this language by describing the virginal conception as the genesis of Jesus.
- Here are three pieces from Haydn's *The Creation*.

Choir: 'Awake the harp'
Choir: 'The heavens are telling'
Choir: 'Achieved is the glorious work' (first chorus)

'Praise the Lord! ye heavens adore him'

- While this tune is often associated with Hitler for its pairing with the words '*Deutschland, Deutschland, über alles*', it is in fact a tune written by Haydn. It began life as '*Gott erhalt Franz den Kaiser*' (God save Emperor Franz) in 1797. The first verse of the hymn is a paraphrase of Psalm 148, which shows all of creation praising the Lord.

Hymn: 'Praise the Lord! ye heavens adore him' (Austria)

'Achieved is the glorious work'

- Haydn appended the words 'Praise to God' at the end of every completed composition. He later described how, writing *The Creation*, he fell on his knees each day and begged God to give him the strength to finish it.
- The overall message is the completeness of God's project and the fittingness of every feature: Achieved is the glorious work.

Choir: 'Achieved is the glorious work' (second chorus)

HOPE

And I saw a new heaven

Choir: 'My Lord, what a morning!' – Spiritual arr. H. T. Burleigh (public domain)

Heaven

- There are generally two obsessions about heaven. One is the harrowing anxiety about who gets into heaven and who gets sent to hell, and the determination to do whatever it takes to make sure one's in the group going upstairs rather than downstairs. The other involves offering words of comfort to the bereaved. The tendency is to avoid facing hard theological and philosophical questions in the mistaken notion that one's principal role is to offer comfort, however superficial and clichéd that comfort may be.
- The key moment came in the mid-nineteenth century, when people started to stop believing in hell. This is usually thought to be for moral reasons – that a good God would not dismiss people for ever. But even stronger are the philosophical reasons – that an almighty God could not allow any part of the good creation to become alienated indefinitely. Once the anxiety over rejection began to recede, Christianity was no longer principally about escaping jeopardy and became more about modelling eternal life.
- Heaven is not the continuation of a person's eternal soul. Humans are one in life, body and soul, and one in death, body and soul. (This goes against the familiar words, 'Death is nothing at all. I have only slipped away into the next room … Life … is the same as it ever was. There is absolutely unbroken continuity.') Christian hope lies not in pretending otherwise, but in knowing that our death is not the end of God. Neither is heaven our reabsorption into the infinite. The words, 'I am a thousand winds that blow, I am the diamond glints on snow, I am the sun on ripened grain, I am the gentle autumn rain' come out of a world view that has stopped caring whether a belief is true so long as it's comforting. These quotations make no reference to the scriptural notion of heaven, have no place for God, and specifically have no relationship to anything brought about by Jesus.

'God that madest earth and heaven'

- Reginald Heber approached the Archbishop of Canterbury about the idea of publishing a book of hymns after he had penned 'Brightest and best' in 1815. The archbishop refused his permission, on the grounds that writing hymns was what Methodists did. Heber later became Bishop of Calcutta, at a time when the diocese included Australia, and died in 1823 after a particularly strenuous baptism and confirmation service in the sun. His widow revisited the archbishop in 1827 with a view to the posthumous publication of his hymns and this time received a better answer. This hymn was written after Heber had heard the familiar Welsh tune 'All through the night' and he turned the words into a prayer for protection against all ills. Richard Whately, Archbishop of Dublin, later added an additional verse.

Hymn: 'God that madest earth and heaven' (Ar hyd y nos)

Three anthems

- The book of Revelation was written on the island of Patmos, 60 miles south-west of Turkey, around 95 CE. Its genre is apocalyptic, and its portrayal of cosmic conflict is almost cartoon-like in its caricatures and contrasts. It marks the beginning of the persecution of the Church and martyrdom. There are plenty of symbolic versions of the transcendent world, and much emphasis on numbers such as 4, 7 and 12. There is dualism between good and evil, light and dark, truth and falsehood, God and Satan. It is set near the end of history as a prelude to final vindication. Edgar Bainton spent much of his life in Newcastle except during World War One, when he was interned in Ruhleben. He moved to Sydney, Australia to be director of the New South Wales State Conservatorium. 'And I saw a new heaven' is his classic treatment of Revelation 21, for which he is most remembered.
- Samuel Barber was born in Pennsylvania in 1910. He earned the most enduring fame of any twentieth-century American composer. In Gerard Manley Hopkins' poem 'Heaven-haven', a nun takes the veil seeking sanctuary from the travails and perils of earthly life.
- 'Faire is the heaven' is a 1925 setting by the long-time Director of Music of St George's Chapel, Windsor, William Harris, of a 1596 poem by Edward Spenser entitled 'An Hymn of Heavenly Beauty'. Harris selected lines from three stanzas of a poem over 40 stanzas in length. This is often described as one of the best-loved works in the Anglican repertoire.

Choir: 'And I saw a new heaven' – Edgar Bainton (RSCM)
Choir: 'Heaven-haven' – Samuel Barber (Schirmer)
Choir: 'Faire is the heaven' – William Harris (Banks Music Publications)

'Jerusalem the golden'

- This hymn is based on a 3,000-line satirical poem by Bernard of Cluny, '*De Contemptu Mundi*', which was translated by the redoubtable Victorian hymnodist J. M. Neale. Bernard's 'On Contempt for the World' included priests, nuns, bishops, monks and Rome itself, all of which are mercilessly scourged for their shortcomings. It consequently became a favourite Protestant text after Reformation. Bernard of Cluny was a twelfth-century French Benedictine monk. '*De Contemptu*' is about the transitory character of all material pleasures and the permanency of spiritual joys, and contains vivid pictures of heaven and hell. S. S. Wesley wrote 'Aurelia' for this hymn, but that tune became associated with 'The Church's one Foundation'; instead it is now sung to 'Ewing' by the Scottish nineteenth-century soldier Alexander Ewing.

Hymn: 'Jerusalem the golden' (Ewing)

'Let the heaven light shine on me'

- By the time of his early death at 45 from a brain tumour, Moses Hogan was considered the world's greatest arranger of spiritual music. He published 88 vocal arrangements. He was born in New Orleans and grew up in a choir led by his uncle. He was also an accomplished painter.

Choir: 'Let the heaven light shine on me' – Spiritual arr. Moses Hogan (Hal Leonard)

Lord of all hopefulness: Lord of all joy

Choir: 'Morning has broken' – Philip Stopford (Hal Leonard)

Joy

- This is the first of four reflections that consider Jan Struther's hymn, 'Lord of all hopefulness'. C. S. Lewis calls joy 'an unsatisfied desire which is itself more desirable than any other satisfaction'. This joy is distinguished from happiness or pleasure. There are 400 references to joy in the Bible. Most famously Nehemiah 8 asserts 'the joy of the Lord is your strength' and Psalm 51 entreats 'restore to me the joy of your salvation'. Joy is a by-product of seeking God: it is God's gift rather than our achievement. As Lewis also says, 'Aim for heaven and you get earth thrown in. Aim for earth and you get neither.' Joy is what creation was made for: it is the 'very good' that God identified after each day of creation.

- Joy is much associated with the coming of Jesus: John the Baptist leaps in his mother's womb, and the angels proclaim good news of great joy. Jesus describes heavenly joy – a shepherd finding his lost sheep, a woman finding a coin, the angels at a penitent sinner, the work of the disciples on mission. All leads towards the joy of the last day: hope is an anticipation of the final joy of heaven.

'Awake my soul, and with the sun'

- Thomas Ken was an orphan who was raised by Izaak Walton, who wrote *The Compleat Angler*. He became chaplain to Charles II, but frowned upon Charles' amorous adventures. On one occasion when the king asked to visit with Nell Gwyn, he said, 'Not for your kingdom would I allow such an insult on the house of a royal chaplain.' Ken was made Bishop of Bath and Wells in 1685 and ministered to Charles as he lay dying. He refused to sign a document enabling James II, as a Roman Catholic, to remain king, but somewhat contrarily then also refused to swear allegiance to William III, having already done so to James – thus becoming a non-juror, and losing his bishopric. He lived out his days at Longleat House. He was buried at sunrise at Frome, Somerset, with this hymn being used at the service.
- He wrote 'Awake my soul, and with the sun' in 1674 before his ascent to royal favour, while still a chaplain at Winchester School. It is most often sung to Morning Hymn, which was written by Francois Bathelemon in 1685 at the request of the chaplain of a girls' orphanage in London. Like the hymn with which Ken partnered it, 'Glory to thee my God this night', it can also be sung to Tallis' Canon.

Hymn: 'Awake my soul, and with the sun' (Morning Hymn)

Three anthems

- 'O radiant dawn' is an Advent antiphon – one of the seven associated with the hymn 'O come O come Emmanuel'. It was written by James MacMillan as part of the Strathclyde Motets in 2007.
- Bob Chilcott's 'This day' comes from a Hebrew text. The unison section explores three dimensions of God's favour, in the call on God to strengthen, bless and lift those who offer praise. Then intriguingly it concludes with the words 'visit us for good'. It's a phrase that appeals equally to Jews, for whom the Messiah has not come but the blessings the Messiah will bring are still deeply sought, and Christians, for whom the Messiah has come, and the prayer is for the Holy Spirit to bring to God's people the blessings already given in Christ.
- Lucy Walker's 'Today' invites us into a scene of light and glorious harmony. It is a setting of a verse by Ozioma Ogbaji, a Nigerian poet and visual storyteller,

and the screenwriter behind the romantic comedy success *Kambili: The Whole 30 Yards*. The poem goes, 'Today I rise, I soar in splendour As the day keeps unveiling all her grandeur Let the chains of yesterday break away! Today is here, I will not cling to yesterday!' Lucy Walker is composer in residence at St Martin-in-the-Fields.

Choir: 'O radiant dawn' – James MacMillan (Boosey & Hawkes)
Choir: 'This day' – Bob Chilcott (Oxford University Press)
Choir: 'Today' – Lucy Walker (Graphite Publishing)

'Today I awake and God is before me'

- The hymn 'Today I awake and God is before me' was written in 1989 by John Bell and Graham Maule, and goes to the tune 'Slithers of Gold' – whose title is taken from a line in the first verse of the hymn. The hymn begins by echoing Jacob's dream of the ladder of angels, and his awakening with the words, 'This is the gate of heaven.' Echoing St Patrick's Breastplate, subsequent verses begin 'Today I arise and Christ is beside me', 'Today I affirm the Spirit within me', 'Today I enjoy the Trinity round me'.

Hymn: 'Today I awake and God is before me' (Slithers of Gold)

'My spirit sang all day'

- In 'My spirit sang all day', poet laureate Robert Bridges portrays the intense experience of joy. Gerald Finzi chose it for arranging because it mentions the word 'joy' a dozen times – and Finzi's wife was called Joy.

Choir: 'My spirit sang all day' – Gerald Finzi (Boosey & Hawkes)

Lord of all hopefulness: Lord of all faith

Choir: 'O Lord, increase our faith' – Loosemore (public domain)

'Lord of all faith'

- This is the second of four reflections that consider Jan Struther's hymn, 'Lord of all hopefulness'. Jan Struther (1901–53) was the pen name of Joyce Placzek,

née Torrens, whose mother's maiden name was Anstruther, and who wrote *Mrs Miniver*, which became a 1942 American romantic war film portraying how the life of an unassuming British housewife in rural England was touched by World War Two. The film won six Academy Awards, and is ranked number 40 on the American Film Institute's list celebrating the most inspirational films of all time. Anstruther was an agnostic churchgoer who suffered from severe depression. She also wrote 'When a knight won his spurs'. The chief significance of this hymn is that it was the first to address God as 'you' rather than 'thou'. The hymn was written in 1931 to match the tune 'Slane' at the request of Percy Dearmer for his collection *Songs of Praise*. The four verses refer to morning, noon, evening and night. Cyril Taylor composed a tune specially for this hymn, appropriately called 'Miniver'.
- For Aristotle, the cardinal virtues were courage, justice, prudence (wisdom) and temperance (moderation). But based on Paul's closing words in 1 Corinthians 13, Augustine and Thomas Aquinas added three more theological virtues – faith, hope and love. We may think of faith as referring to the conviction about things revealed in the past, hope as looking with confidence to the future, and love as living in the present in the light of a healed past and secure future.

'Affirm anew the threefold Name'

- This was written by the prolific Anglican hymnwriter and bishop, Timothy Dudley-Smith, for the Lambeth Conference of Anglican bishops in 1998. It takes the fourfold theme of the conference across four verses: affirm, declare, confirm, renew. Dudley-Smith wrote it at home at Ford near Salisbury in September 1996.

Hymn: 'Affirm anew the threefold Name' (Saint Matthew)

Three anthems

- Orlando Gibbons' anthem 'Almighty and everlasting God' is a setting of the collect for Epiphany 3 from the Book of Common Prayer. The text goes 'Almighty and everlasting God, mercifully look upon our infirmities, and in all our dangers and necessities stretch forth thy right hand to help and defend us; through Jesus Christ our Lord.' The prayer book collects all have the same shape: an address to God, an account of what we know about God that invites us to seek help (missing here), a specific request ('look upon … stretch forth') expressed in an imperative verb, an account of the result of answered prayer (missing here), and a concluding route for the petition ('through Jesus …'). They thus combine faith in the past and hope for the future.
- Martin How's father was first Rector of Liverpool Parish Church and then Bishop of Glasgow and Galloway, so young Martin grew up in Scotland. He

spent much of his life working for the Royal School of Church Music and died in 2022. 'Day by day', which is based on the famous prayer of St Richard of Chichester, is How's best-known composition. The prayer to see God more clearly, love God more dearly and follow God more nearly echoes a stirring Sufi prayer: 'God of time and eternity, if I love thee for hope of heaven, then deny me heaven; if I love thee for fear of hell, then give me hell; but if I love thee for thyself alone, then give me thyself alone.'
- Henry Alford was a nineteenth-century Dean of Canterbury. He wrote this hymn for the season of Ascension, when the disciples can no longer see Jesus, yet still love him. This season balances the doubt of Thomas with the burning hearts of the disciples on the road to Emmaus. Alford looks forward to the day when we shall see Christ face to face. Lloyd Larson is a contemporary American composer who lives in Minnesota.

Choir: 'Almighty and everlasting God' – Orlando Gibbons (public domain, published in *The Oxford Book of Tudor Anthems*, OUP)
Choir: 'Day by day' – Martin How (RSCM)
Choir: 'We walk by faith' – Lloyd Larson (Beckenhorst Press)

'The love of God comes close'

- This hymn by John Bell and Graham Maule of the Iona Community makes connections between the singer and those in need of God's love, peace, joy and grace. On the way the singers perceive their own need for love, peace, joy and grace. In the final verse we discover that these are embodied in Jesus. Jesus draws close to us and 'is here to stay, embracing those who walk his way'. It can be sung to Bell's own tune 'Melanie', or to 'Love Unknown'.

Hymn: 'The love of God comes close' (Melanie)

'Ain'a that good news'

- This African American spiritual elides the distinction between faith and joy, evoking William Wordsworth's expression, 'surprised by joy'. This is how C. S. Lewis speaks of faith and joy at the conclusion of his book whose name comes from Wordsworth's expression: 'When we are lost in the woods the sight of a signpost is a great matter. He who first sees it cries, "Look!" The whole party gathers round and stares. But when we have found the road and are passing signposts every few miles, we shall not stop and stare. They will encourage us and we shall be grateful to the authority that set them up. But we shall not stop and stare, or not much; not on this road, though their pillars are of silver and their lettering of gold.'

Choir: 'Ain'a that good news' – Spiritual arr. William Dawson (Neil A. Kjos Music Company)

Lord of all hopefulness: Lord of all grace

Choir: 'O Holy Spirit, Lord of grace' – Christopher Tye (public domain)

Grace

- There are two great divides on the theology of grace. The first is between the Western and Eastern Church. The Western notion centres on the Fall, which creates a predicament that humankind face guilt and mortality. Grace comes in the form of Jesus, who redeems sin through forgiveness and transforms mortality through the Resurrection. The Eastern notion places much more emphasis on God's original purpose in creation, allowing that creation was made so that God could be with us in Christ, and maintaining that Christ would have come even had there not been a fall. Thus grace lies in God's original purpose.
- The second great divide is between Catholics and Protestants. The Catholic view is that the Holy Spirit works through the Church, and specifically through the sacraments, to provide for believers the means of grace. Bridging figures like Luther and Wesley maintain that grace comes through preaching and sacraments. But Calvinists traditionally hold to the notion of irresistible grace, through which the Holy Spirit enlivens those whose sin makes them fail to seek God's grace. A common way of putting it is God's Redemption At Christ's Expense.
- All parties see grace as a free and glorious gift and perhaps the most distinctive characteristic of God, which humankind does nothing to earn.

'God of mercy, God of grace'

- This hymn was written by H. F. Lyte, Scottish Episcopalian and author of 'Abide with me'. It was first published in 1834 in his *Spirit of the Psalms*, as his second version of Psalm 67. It is often sung as a harvest hymn ('earth shall then its fruits afford') but is also suitable for the transfiguration, as the second line, 'Show the brightness of thy face', indicates.

Hymn: 'God of mercy, God of grace' (Heathlands)

Three anthems

- The line 'Be there at our homing' from the third verse of 'Lord of all hopefulness' is part of a sequence – waking, labours, homing and sleeping – that pervades the hymn. Home is a significant theme in the Bible: it begins with Adam and Eve cast out from their perfect home, and moves to Abraham being promised a home. Joshua enters that home but it is occupied by others; finally, Saul and David make it a home for God's people for ever; but it doesn't last long, and exile is the fate of those who sought home. Some Jews find a home in the diaspora, but Ezra and Nehemiah resurrect the notion of home. Yet for 500 years the Jews' home is ruled by others. In Jesus comes the notion that here we have no abiding city and our true home lies elsewhere. His resurrection offers a route there. Lucy Walker's 'Here, home' is a characteristically deft and subtle gesture towards many meanings of home in a world where many are displaced or homeless.
- In George Herbert's 'Love bade me welcome', the scene is a banquet, to which the poet is invited. But he holds back, afraid of going in. Love continues to invite, asking the poet's reason for withdrawing. The poet says he's not worthy. Love insists the poet is worthy. The poet continues to doubt. Love takes the poet's hand and reels off terms of endearment. The poet continues to draw back. Love continues to turn the tables on the poet. The poet, like the prodigal son, says I will come and serve, but love says no, I will serve you, and the poet finally gives in. It is a classic portrayal of grace. Geoff Weaver is an accomplished musician who directed music for the Lambeth Conference in 1988.
- Psalm 84 is about a journey. It describes the hopes of a pilgrim walking to Jerusalem, both on the way there and the way back. In one complex and disputed line, it suggests that the tears shed on the way there may be used as a well on the way home. Johannes Brahms uses it as part of his German Requiem, first performed in 1868, inspired by the death of his mother and perhaps also that of Robert Schumann.

Choir: 'Here, home' – Lucy Walker (Lucy Walker)
Choir: 'Love bade me welcome' – Geoff Weaver (RSCM)
Choir: 'How lovely are thy dwellings' (from A German Requiem) – Johannes Brahms (public domain, published by Novello)

'Let us build a house'

- This song was written for a church dedication: but it clearly speaks of church as a place of grace and hospitality, a true home of God, with the constant repetition of the refrain, All are welcome. Its simple tune hides some aspirational language – 'rock of faith and vault of grace'; and the final lines summarize the purpose of church – end divisions, claim the faith, share the feast, end fear and danger. Marty Haugen is a contemporary American songwriter shaped in the Lutheran tradition.

Hymn: 'Let us build a house' (Marty Haugen)

'Amazing grace'

- John Newton grew up without any particular religious conviction. He was involuntarily forced into service in the Royal Navy and, after leaving the service, he became involved in the Atlantic slave trade. In 1748, a violent storm battered his vessel off the coast of County Donegal, Ireland so strongly that he called out to God for mercy. He survived the storm and while his boat was being repaired he wrote the first verse of this famous song. He continued his slave trading career, however, for another 20 years. 'Amazing grace' was used extensively during the Second Great Awakening in the early nineteenth century. It can be seen as an example of the power of grace to transform lives, as in the film *Amazing Grace* about William Wilberforce and the end of slavery, but also as the way grace can be confined to a transformation of the soul, with no apparent change of life, as in Newton's story, at least initially.

Choir: 'Amazing grace' – arr. Will Todd (Boosey & Hawkes)

Lord of all hopefulness: Lord of all calm

Choir: 'Sure on this shining night' (SATB) – Samuel Barber (Schirmer)

'The end of the day'

- The significance of the evening hour in Christian thought and devotion has perhaps never been better expressed than by the spiritual writer and priest Jim Cotter, who died in 2014. Here he adapts an evening collect: 'O living God, in Jesus Christ you were laid in the tomb at an evening hour, and so sanctified the grave to be a bed of hope to your people. Give us courage and faith to die daily to our sin and pride, that even as this flesh and blood decays, our lives may still grow in you, that at our last day our dying may be done so well that we live in you for ever. Amen.'
- When Thomas Cranmer, seeking to produce a liturgy for common prayer, in other words not just for monks and nuns, resolved the offices of vespers and

Compline into Evensong, he was shaping the imagination of ordinary disciples to bind the day with psalms and Scripture readings. His best-known evening prayer goes, 'Lighten our darkness, we beseech thee, O Lord; and by thy great mercy defend us from all perils and dangers of this night; for the love of thy only Son, our Saviour Jesus Christ.'
- Ignatius Loyola instructed Jesuits to practise what he called the Examen each evening, in five steps: 1. Become aware of God's presence. 2. Review the day with gratitude. 3. Pay attention to your emotions. 4. Choose one feature of the day and pray from it. 5. Look towards tomorrow.

'Before the ending of the day'

- The office of Compline comes from the notion of completing the day. It is first mentioned in The Rule of St Benedict around 500. Some trace it back to Basil the Great in the fourth century. Even though Cranmer combined Vespers and Compline to make Evensong, Compline reappeared in the 1928 Prayer Book. It is usually sung unaccompanied.
- Before the ending of the day is J. M. Neale's translation of the ancient hymn 'Te lucis ante terminum'.

Hymn: 'Before the ending of the day' (Plainsong)

Three anthems

- 'Hail, gladdening light' is one of the oldest Christian hymns to survive complete. It was not a congregational hymn but was for the lighting of the lamps at sunset in the home. It is a hymn of praise to the Holy Trinity and especially to Christ as the Light of the World. The original was not written in verses of repeating metre and the translation by John Keble (1792–1866) has kept that, making it impossible to set an ordinary hymn tune to these words. Charles Wood was an Irish composer who numbered Ralph Vaughan Williams and Herbert Howells among his pupils.
- 'Creator of the stars of night' is another ancient Latin hymn translated by J. M. Neale. It is sometimes credited to St Ambrose. In a very short space – four verses before a doxology – the hymn traces the whole of salvation history, through creation, fall, incarnation and on to the last day.
- Annabel Rooney's setting of William Romanis' hymn 'Round me falls the night' creates a suitably ethereal atmosphere. The hymn is a brief but comprehensive review of the evening themes of Christian devotion: darkness as mystery, through which Jesus shines clearly; evening as ending, with Jesus assuring his constancy; the premonition of death, with Jesus as the love that will not let me go. Romanis

was a Victorian clergyman who served in Reading and Leicestershire. Annabel Rooney is an emerging composer based in Devon, who also excels as a cellist.

Choir: 'Hail, gladdening light' – Charles Wood (public domain, published by OUP)
Choir: 'Creator of the stars of night' – Plainsong arr. John Scott (OUP)
Choir: 'Round me falls the night' – Annabel Rooney (OUP)

'The day thou gavest'

- 'The day thou gavest' looks like an evening hymn but is actually a celebration of the spread of Christianity around the British empire. It was printed in Ellerton's 1871 book *Church Hymns* (a rival to *Hymns Ancient & Modern*). It was inspired by 1 Chronicles 23.30 – 'their office was to stand every morning to thank and praise the Lord, and likewise at even' – and Psalm 113.3: 'From the rising of the sun to the going down of the same the Lord's name is to be praised.'
- The hymn begins with Genesis and ends with Revelation. It starts with God giving light and ends with all creatures worshipping at God's throne. It begins and ends in church, but in the middle it describes the planet spinning into space and encompasses people across the empire. In the end the empire is transcended by the kingdom of God – but the two come close to being identified.
- It was chosen for Queen Victoria's diamond jubilee in 1897. The tune by Arthur Sullivan, the second half of Gilbert and Sullivan, was regarded as too waltz-like by the *English Hymnal*, but marvellously captures the sweep of the words.

Hymn: 'The day thou gavest' (St Clement)

'The long day closes'

- 'The long day closes' was written in 1868 by Henry Fothergill Chorley with music by Arthur Sullivan. It became Sullivan's best-known song for four parts. Part songs were catching on in Victorian England due to the growth of choral societies. The song is an extended meditation on death. It speaks of the words of mirth being now dumb for ever. Its most famous line is 'Hope believes and fate disposes'. The song gave its name to a 1992 film about the impoverishment of post-war domestic life, focused on church, school and family relationships.

Choir: 'The long day closes' – Arthur Sullivan (public domain, published by Novello)

FAITH

The Word of the Lord

Choir: 'Open thou mine eyes' – John Rutter (Oxford University Press)

The Bible

- The Bible is above all a story. We can understand that story as a five-act play. The first act is creation. There was too much love in the Trinity for God not to share it. The world is not the centre of the story: God is. Things do not have to be the way they are – they exist because God chose for them to be. God says, 'I made you this way because I wanted one like you.' Their chief purpose is to glorify and enjoy God for ever. And yet these creatures use their freedom ill. They choose, but have lost the art of making good choices. Here is the drama of creation, of how God came to turn infinite divine freedom into a covenant, and how humanity comes to turn finite created freedom into a prison.
- The second act is Israel. God longed to be in true relationship with humankind. This failed in Adam and failed again at Babel. So God called Abraham. The rest of the Old Testament is a love story, in which Israel strives with God, unable to live with God and unable to live without God. Can Israel find the forms of life that honour its call to be holy? How will God woo or wrest Israel back when Israel strays? How far is too far to stray?
- The third act is Jesus. Here the drama is at its most stark. Is God totally vulnerable, or is there something kept back? Will God's people understand, comprehend and follow, or will they seek to overcome, stand over, obliterate and annihilate? Will their rejection of God cause God's rejection of them?
- Christians are in act four, the Church. In this act, the Church is given all it needs to continue to be Christ's body in the world. It receives the Holy Spirit and is clothed with power and authority. It is given the Scripture. It is given baptism, a way in which to incorporate people into the drama. It is given the Eucharist, a regular event in which the body of Christ meets the embodied Christ. It is given other practices to form and sustain its life. Will those gifts prove to be enough? Will the Church seek solace elsewhere? This is the drama of the present moment, of every moment in the Church's history.

- Still to come is act five, the end. This is a frightening thing for those who have built up power and resources, but for those who have nothing to lose it is unbounded joy. The drama of that time may yield some shocks as the secrets of all hearts are revealed. But in God's revelation there will be no shocks, only surprises. For the God who will then be fully revealed will not be different in character from the God who was revealed in act three. The face on the cross will be the face on the throne.

'God has spoken – by his prophets'

- George Wallace Briggs was a long-time Canon of Worcester. He wrote one of the prayers used at the time of the meeting of Churchill and Roosevelt on HMS *Prince of Wales* in 1941 when the Atlantic Charter was framed. Along with this hymn he is also known for 'Christ is the world's true light' and 'Now is eternal life'.

Hymn: 'God has spoken – by his prophets' (Ebenezer)

Three anthems

- 'Thy word is a lantern' was written by the late seventeenth-century composer Henry Purcell, combining texts from Psalm 119. Psalm 119 is by far the longest psalm and is an extended meditation on what it means to read the Scriptures and to wait upon the word of the Lord. Perhaps the most celebrated such waiting is that of the child Samuel, who three times mistook the word of the Lord for the words of his mentor Eli, but was finally taught by Eli to respond, 'Speak, Lord, for your servant is listening.'
- 'How lovely are the messengers' was written in 1836 by Felix Mendelssohn for his oratorio St Paul. He based it on Romans 10.15, 18.
- Bob Chilcott's 'If ye love me' is based on the words of John 14.15–17: 'If ye love me, keep my commandments. And I will pray the Father, and he shall give you another Comforter, that he may abide with you for ever; Even the spirit of truth'. This is how Jesus connects his own incarnation both to the Old Testament, represented by the commandments, fulfilled but not superseded by Jesus' own injunctions, and to the coming of the Holy Spirit.

Choir: 'Thy word is a lantern' – Henry Purcell (public domain, published by Novello)
Choir: 'How lovely are the messengers' – Felix Mendelssohn (public domain, published by Novello)
Choir: 'If ye love me' – Bob Chilcott (OUP)

'Thanks to God whose word was spoken'

- Reginald Thomas Brooks was a URC minister who worked extensively with the BBC. He wrote this hymn in 1954 for the 150th anniversary of the Bible Society. Brooks explains the various meanings of the 'word of God'; the creative word making the earth, the incarnate word glorifying human flesh, the written word, the Holy Scriptures; and the preached word, through which God is speaking today.

Hymn: 'Thanks to God whose word was spoken' (St Helen)

'The Word was God'

- This anthem is written in an almost spiritual style, with the layering of one sound upon another. Rosephanye Powell was born in 1962 in Lanett, Alabama and is now Professor of Voice at Auburn University. She composes sacred and secular works and has been included in *Who's Who Among America's Teachers and Outstanding Young Women in America*.

Choir: 'The Word was God' – Rosephanye Powell (Gentry Publications)

The Lord's my Shepherd

Choir: 'The Lord's my Shepherd' – Franz Schubert (public domain, published in *European Sacred Music*, OUP)

'The Lord's my Shepherd'

- Psalm 23 is the definitive, but not the only, place where the relationship between God and God's people is likened to that of a shepherd and a flock of sheep. The psalm speaks of ten joys. 'He makes me lie down in green pastures' indicates abundant life in a dry Middle Eastern land. 'He leads me beside still waters' suggests cold, fresh, flowing water in a parched landscape. 'He restores my soul' portrays God as like an old friend who brings us back to life. 'He leads me in right paths for his name's sake' tells us God wants the best for us. 'Even though I walk through the valley of the shadow of death, I fear no evil; for you are with me' stresses the companionship of the God that never leaves us, even at the worst moments. 'Your rod and your staff – they comfort me' assures us that

God is not going to run away. 'You prepare a table before me in the presence of my enemies' is an extraordinary statement of peace, invariably understood by Christians as pointing to the Eucharist. 'You anoint my head with oil' anticipates the anonymous woman in Bethany – except it's a representation of God. 'My cup overflows' is often taken as a depiction of the heavenly banquet. Finally, 'Surely goodness and mercy shall follow me all the days of my life' is perhaps most remarkable of all: these are not things we pursue – they pursue us.

'Abide with me'

- This is a hymn that moves from earthly darkness to heavenly light. It's possible it was inspired by the poetry of Henry Vaughan, who wrote 'My soul, there is a country', since the hymn's author H. F. Lyte edited an edition of Vaughan's poems. It was written shortly before the end of Lyte's life. He died in Nice in 1847.
- The central imagery is that of the disciples' invitation to Jesus, as evening fell on the road to Emmaus, to abide with them. Lyte makes the request singular and thus more intense. The day is ending – but the day is Easter Day, a day that never ends. But there remain some similar themes to the 23rd Psalm: Jesus has pursued the disciples, not vice versa; he has led them in right paths; he has restored their soul; he sets a table in their sight. In all, the parallels are significant.
- The tune was written by W. H. Monk, musical editor of *Hymns Ancient & Modern*. The principal theme of the fourth movement of Gustav Mahler's Ninth Symphony echoes this tune. The first and last verses have been sung at the FA Cup final and Rugby League Challenge Cup Final at Wembley since the 1920s. The hymn was played by the band as the *Titanic* was sinking.

Hymn: 'Abide with me' (Eventide)

Three anthems

- The Jewish baritone Gerald Cohen composed a Hebrew setting of Psalm 23 in 1992. Cohen has spent most of his life in New York. His music draws together the Western tradition of Brahms, Bartok and Britten with his own Jewish roots. He is best known for a setting of Psalm 43. He has written operas about love in a concentration camp and the relationship between Sarah and Hagar in the book of Genesis.
- 'He shall feed his flock' is a rare element of Handel's *Messiah* that appears to refer to Jesus' earthly ministry. In fact, the words are taken from Isaiah 40 – almost all the references to Jesus in *The Messiah* are Old Testament ones. The

- piece is matched with 'Come unto me all ye who labour and are heavy laden', which actually does come from the Gospels – Matthew 11.
- Karl Jenkins is among the most performed composers in the world today. He is best known for his *The Armed Man: A Mass for Peace*. 'The Shepherd' is a poem from William Blake's *Songs of Innocence*. The poem is like a commentary on Psalm 23: equally short, and clearly echoing the psalm in lines like 'He shall follow his sheep all the day', and 'He is watchful while they are in peace'.

Choir: '*Adonai ro'i lo echsar* (Psalm 23)' – Gerald Cohen (www.geraldcohenmusic.com)
Choir: 'He shall feed his flock' (from *The Messiah*) – George Frideric Handel (public domain, published by OUP, Novello and others)
Choir: 'The Shepherd' – Karl Jenkins (Boosey & Hawkes)

'The King of love my shepherd is'

- This setting of Psalm 23 concludes with the line 'Within thy house for ever.' It's a fitting sentiment not just to describe the Christian hope to dwell with God eternally but the lifetime of service given by the hymn's author Sir Henry Baker, the editor of *Hymns Ancient & Modern*, who spoke the words of the third verse on his deathbed. It appeared in the 1867 appendix. One interesting alteration from the psalm is that the shepherd sets a table 'in my sight': the original reference to enemies has disappeared.
- The editors of *Hymns Ancient & Modern* refused permission for the compilers of the *English Hymnal* to use the original tune 'Dominus Regit Me', so Vaughan Williams set it to St Columba.

Hymn: 'The King of love my shepherd is' (University)

'All we like sheep'

- What the story in Luke 15 picks up that is less evident in Psalm 23 is the tendency of sheep to wander off and need rescuing. This theme has played a huge part in Christian reflection on sheep, and is the subject of Luke's parable. It does feature in Handel's *Messiah* in a section derived from the fourth song of the suffering servant in Isaiah 53.

Choir: 'All we like sheep' (from *The Messiah*) – George Frideric Handel (public domain, published by OUP and Novello)

Justice

Choir: 'Give me justice' – James MacMillan (Boosey & Hawkes)

Justice

- There are broadly three kinds of justice. The first is constructive: it's about judgement, and about a whole body of laws and precedents that, together with traditions, punishments and professional standards, constitute a legal system. The second underwrites the first: it's about the rule of law, about building institutions in civil society, ensuring freedom of the press, and maintaining a strong ethic of public service – which together create a law-abiding culture. But the justice of good order has little will and almost no capacity to redistribute power, and it's in unequal distribution of power that a great deal of injustice actually lies. Justice also has to mean, third, some degree of redistribution of power, restoration of what misfortune has taken away, and re-creation of opportunity for those denied it. It's about giving a first chance to all who've grown up in the prison of poverty, disease and disadvantage, and a second chance to any who've made mistakes and are eager to learn from them.

'The kingdom of God is justice and joy'

- In 'The kingdom of God is justice and joy', Bryn Rees characterizes God's kingdom in four ways – as justice and joy, as mercy and grace, as challenge and choice, and as gift and goal – thereby overcoming the tendency to bifurcate the faith as understood either as salvation eternally or liberation temporally. While the outcast is welcomed, there is a conventional theology of the atonement: God's love for us sinners brought Christ to his cross. Bryn Rees was a twentieth-century Congregationalist minister who wrote the words for several compositions by William Lloyd Webber, father of Andrew.

Hymn: 'The kingdom of God is justice and joy' (Hanover)

Three anthems

- As soon as you see a motet in Latin you know that this was one William Byrd wrote for private use by Catholics – while he was still composing anthems in English for public worship after the Reformation. His subtle game of survival as a state- and church-sponsored musician is also visible in his sly political references: when a line says Zion has become a wasteland, Jerusalem a desolation, the original text from Isaiah 64.10–11 refers to the Jews' exile in Babylon, but Byrd is fully aware that Catholics (known at this time as recusants) would perceive it as a comment on the state of Protestant England. This is a double motet, composed of two symmetrical parts. Part one is the exiles' plea for divine mercy; Part two is the exiles' lament over the loss of the holy city. Today it makes a fitting lament over any dwelling place that has become a wasteland.

- The Beatitudes in Matthew 5 have been called the most important words spoken by the most important person who ever lived. They comprise nine blessings for behaviours of marginalized people: God overcomes the empire of power, status and wealth with quiet subversion. They come alive when you realize Jesus is describing his own life: this is Jesus' autobiography. One can read the first half of each beatitude as the cross and the second half as the Resurrection – and today's Church as dwelling in the comma between the two.
- Edith Cavell was a British nurse from Norfolk. At the age of 42 she became matron of a major nursing school in Brussels. She became one of the most influential nurses in Belgium. At the outbreak of war she was with her mother in Norfolk but she courageously returned to Brussels and worked with the Red Cross. From November 1914 she started sheltering British and French soldiers who sought to return home and Belgians who sought to escape the German occupation. All told, she helped 200 Allied soldiers escape from German-occupied Belgium during World War One, for which she was court-martialled, found guilty of treason and sentenced to death. Edith Piaf, born two months later, was named after her. Cecilia McDowell composed 'Standing as I do before God' in 2013, a setting of Seán Street's reflection on words spoken by Cavell on the eve of her execution on 12 October 1915. Recorded by the Anglican chaplain Stirling Graham, her last words were: 'Patriotism is not enough: I must have no hatred or bitterness towards anyone.' These words are engraved below her statue, which stands in St Martin's Place, near Trafalgar Square, in London.

Choir: '*Ne irascaris Domine*' – William Byrd (public domain, published by OUP)
Choir: 'The Beatitudes' – Philip Stopford (MorningStar Music Publishers)
Choir: 'Standing as I do before God' – Cecilia McDowall (OUP)

'Jesus Christ is waiting'

- John Bell and Graham Maule wrote this hymn to the tune of a traditional French carol dating from the late fifteenth to the early sixteenth century. The tune is familiar from its pairing with the Easter hymn 'Now the green blade riseth'. The hymn engages some of the deepest passions of Jesus' ministry, including rage, and sees the work of the Holy Spirit in those who embody Jesus' passion today.

Hymn: 'Jesus Christ is waiting' (Noël Nouvelet)

'All my trials, Lord'

- The origin of this song is unclear – it has been described as a white spiritual that gained a Caribbean flavour in the Bahamas. It was first released commercially in 1956 and became associated with the protests of the era, being included in the *Joan Baez Songbook* in 1964. Like many spirituals, it sees trials as a condition of this life and a crossing-over to liberty as imminent.

Choir: 'All my trials, Lord' – Spiritual arr. Bob Chilcott (OUP)

Prayer

Choir: 'With prayer and supplication' – Amy Beach (public domain)

Prayer

- Prayer is consciousness of being in the presence of God. To be in the presence of God is humanity's purpose and destiny. The whole of the Christian life is training for enjoying the presence of God. The sense of being so united with God that we are almost in God while at the same time being so aware of God that we are deeply with God is what we call communion. Prayer can be experienced alone or with intimate and like-minded companions, or in public worship. There are traditionally four parts of prayer: adoration, confession, thanksgiving and supplication.
- Prayer is a conversation between the Son and the Father in which the Holy Spirit invites the believer to participate. Christians imagine heaven as a place where the members of the Holy Trinity are surrounded by the angels and saints in glory. The Holy Spirit is constantly bringing the prayers of the angels and saints to the Son, and the Son is constantly pleading those petitions to the Father. That's why prayer is appropriately described as joining the praise of God by the angels and saints that is going on all the time.
- The Son who pleads with the Father on our behalf is always the Jesus we see on the cross. Every petition is, on closer scrutiny, a plea for safety, healing, reconciliation, communion, blessing – for all the things Christ displayed on the cross. So every time the Holy Spirit carries our prayer to Jesus and Jesus intercedes to the Father for us, the question for the Father is the same: 'How much of your ultimate glory are you going to reveal and bestow at this present moment, and how much are you going to withhold until the last day?'

'Father, hear the prayer we offer'

- This American hymn was published in a monthly magazine in 1859 by Maria Willis. It was later included in a Unitarian hymn book. Maria Willis was the wife of a doctor in Rochester, New York. Her hymn elaborates on the notion that God helps those who help themselves: we should tread rejoicingly the steep and rugged pathway rather than simply expect to dwell in green pastures beside still waters, as in the imagery of Psalm 23. The tune 'Sussex' is a traditional English melody, arranged by Vaughan Williams.

Hymn: 'Father, hear the prayer we offer' (Sussex)

Three anthems

- Thomas Tallis was a Roman Catholic who served four monarchs as he carefully navigated the hazards of the Reformation and with William Byrd created the English anthem, as so many texts now needed to be set in English. 'Hear the voice and prayer' comes from Solomon's dedicatory prayers over the Temple of Jerusalem in 2 Chronicles 6.19–21.
- 'Hear my prayer' is a setting of Psalm 102 by Henry Purcell. Purcell was an English composer who fused Italian and French styles in his music. No other native-born English composer approached his fame until Edward Elgar. He was born in 1659 close to Westminster Abbey. He attended Westminster School. He wrote music for the coronation of King James II, a birthday ode for Queen Mary, two elegies for Queen Mary II's funeral, *Dido and Aeneas* and many liturgical choral works. He died in 1695 in Dean's Yard, Westminster and is buried adjacent to the organ at Westminster Abbey. His 36-year life spanned the Restoration through to Glorious Revolution – from Puritan to Anglican to Catholic to Protestant.
- Maurice Duruflé published '*Notre Père*', a setting of the Lord's Prayer, in 1977. It was his last published composition, and his only congregational work. Duruflé was organist at Saint-Étienne-du-Mont in Paris and director of the Gregorian Institute. The Lord's Prayer is centrally a prayer about the present (give us), about the past (forgive us) and about the future (deliver us).

Choir: 'Hear the voice and prayer' – Thomas Tallis (public domain)
Choir: 'Hear my prayer' – Henry Purcell (public domain, published by Novello)
Choir: '*Notre Père*' – Maurice Duruflé (Durand)

'Be thou my guardian and my guide'

- This hymn owes much to the Oxford Movement, a high church revival initiated by John Keble and joined by John Henry Newman and Edward Pusey, and hugely influential in liturgical renewal for a hundred years after it began in 1833. Isaac Williams was a prominent member, and wrote this hymn as a meditation on the petition in the Lord's Prayer 'lead us not into temptation'. He was also inspired by Psalm 17.5, 'My steps have held fast to your paths; my feet have not slipped.' Williams wrote two celebrated tracts entitled *On Reserve in Communicating Religious Knowledge* – and this hymn embodies the understatement in which Williams believed. Isaac Smith, who wrote the tune 'Abridge', was an eighteenth-century nonconformist who is thought to have lived in East Anglia, since many of his tunes are named after places in the region. Abridge is a village near Chelmsford in Essex.

Hymn: 'Be thou my guardian and my guide' (Abridge)

'A Prayer of St Columba'

- This is an anthem full of emotion with a dramatic organ part. It was commissioned for a diamond wedding and first performed in 2012. The words go like this: 'Kindle in our hearts, O God, The flame of that love which never ceases, That it may burn in us, giving light to others. May we shine forever in Thy holy temple, Set on fire with Thy eternal light, Even Thy son, Jesus Christ, Our Saviour and Redeemer. Amen.'

Choir: 'A Prayer of St Columba' – Cecilia McDowell (OUP)

I want Jesus to walk with me

Choir: 'You do not walk alone' – Elaine Hagenberg (Beckenhorst Press)

Walking

- The Bible is full of journeys. Abraham walks from Haran to Canaan. Joseph travels in a caravan from Canaan to Egypt. Moses brings the Hebrews back across the wilderness, Joshua brings them into the Promised Land. And so on. In the Middle Ages people started to think of a journey as a quest. A quest is a

- type of journey during which you learn a lot about yourself and your companions but also a lot about the journey you're going on. In other words, your goal isn't really arrival, it's making the most of the journey as a learning and growing experience. It's in that light that it makes sense to think of life as a journey. It's not about ever arriving. It's about taking the time to learn about yourself and your companions, and to reflect on the destination.
- Pilgrimages have three roles in Christianity: they seek supernatural help, they make penance, or they offer thanksgiving. After the conversion of the Emperor Constantine, his mother Helena went to Jerusalem and started a tradition. Pilgrimages set out to Jerusalem, Rome and Santiago de Compostela. From the eighth century, pilgrimage became an alternative to public penance, and thus became a major feature of the Middle Ages.

'I heard the voice of Jesus say'

- The Great Disruption was a schism in 1843 in which 450 evangelical ministers broke away from the 1,200-strong clergy of the Church of Scotland to form the Free Church of Scotland. The main conflict was over whether the Church of Scotland or the British government had the power to control clerical positions and benefits. Reunion didn't take place till 1929 and was only partial.
- Horatio Bonar wrote this hymn shortly before he joined the Free Church schism. Each verse has a specific Gospel text – Matthew 11, John 4, John 8. The tune, 'Kingsfold', was written by Vaughan Williams for the *English Hymnal* in 1906.

Hymn: 'I heard the voice of Jesus say' (Kingsfold)

Three anthems

- 'O for a closer walk with God', like Newman's 'Lead, kindly Light', is a great hymn of faith shrouded in doubt. William Cowper had regular moments of insanity to go with his episodes of clarity. He wrote this hymn in 1769 when he was anxious about the health of his housekeeper, on whom he relied entirely. It was inspired by Genesis 5: Enoch walked with God, and he was not, for God took him. Cowper wrote to a friend of how he fell asleep after writing the first two verses, but then awoke and wrote the third and fourth.
- Will Todd wrote his simple setting of 'Lead me, Lord' for the chapel choir of Durham School in 1997. The words are adapted from Psalm 5. It is a simple prayer for guidance and discernment. The text is most associated with a celebrated setting by S. S. Wesley.

- 'I want Jesus to walk with me' is an African American spiritual. The key word is not so much 'walk' as 'with': it's a prayer for an end to isolation rather than one seeking a solution to a problem.

Choir: 'O for a closer walk with God' – Charles Villiers Stanford (public domain, published by OUP)
Choir: 'Lead me, Lord' – Will Todd (Boosey & Hawkes)
Choir: 'I want Jesus to walk with me' – Spiritual arr. Larry Shackley (Lorenz)

'Guide me, O thou Great Redeemer'

- This hymn is steeped in the Welsh Revival of the eighteenth century. It is soaked in typologies: in Exodus 16 the children of Israel in the barren wilderness land receive the bread of heaven. This is echoed in the bread of life mentioned in John 6. The fire and cloudy pillar guided the children of Israel in Exodus 13. Eventually they crossed the Jordan after 40 years. The Promised Land here represents heaven beyond the death of Jordan.
- The tune '*Cwm Rhondda*' was composed more than 100 years after the hymn, in 1905.

Hymn: 'Guide me, O thou Great Redeemer' (Cwm Rhondda)

'Walk softly'

- The Shaker song 'Walk softly' is about making the most of the journey. The phrase 'walk softly' arose in relation to the room in a Shaker house reserved almost entirely for worship. When Shakers entered the room, they were enjoined to shut doors quietly and walk softly, as they would in the presence of God. The whole scene evokes Moses' encounter with God at the burning bush, where he is told 'Remove the sandals from your feet, for the place on which you are standing is holy ground.' Bob Chilcott's setting of this nineteenth-century Shaker song captures the sense of holiness that might come over all of us when we realize we are entering the presence of the holy and life-giving God.

Choir: 'Walk softly' – Bob Chilcott (OUP)

O for the wings of a dove

Choir: 'All things bright and beautiful' – Philip Stopford (Hal Leonard)

Birds

- There are a wide variety of themes associated with birds in the Bible. There is a lot of concern about being unclean: for example, Goliath threatens David with his flesh being eaten by the birds of the air. In general, birds were a source of food and a cheap meat for sacrifice.
- The Scriptures include many analogies to capture, such as the snare of the fowler in Psalm 91. Wings may be symbols of escape and safety – thus 'oh for the wings of a dove' in Psalm 55. Likewise, Jesus refers to giving shelter under the shadow of his wing like a mother hen. There are a number of moral examples: a dove is a symbol for love many times in Song of Songs, and a sparrow finds itself a nest in God's house in Psalm 84. There are also references to beauty: Solomon collected peacocks.

'Morning has broken'

- This hymn was written in 1931. The words were authored by English writer Eleanor Farjeon, who also wrote 'People, look East' and many children's stories. She was inspired by the village of Alfriston in East Sussex. She set the hymn to a traditional Scottish Gaelic tune known as 'Bunessan'.
- The English pop musician and folk singer Cat Stevens included a version on his 1971 album *Teaser and the Firecat*.

Hymn: 'Morning has broken' (Bunessan)

Three anthems

- 'Morning glory, starlit sky' was originally a poem that forms the epilogue to the theologian W. H. Vanstone's 1977 book *Love's Endeavour, Love's Expense*. Vanstone was greatly influenced by the theology of Dietrich Bonhoeffer's *Letters and Papers from Prison* and the work of Paul Tillich. The book describes his ministry on a postwar housing estate near Manchester and his search for the relevance of Christianity. He reflects on work in this place and of his growing conviction, as he puts it, that 'the love of God must be infinitely more costly, more precarious and more exposed than it is commonly thought to be'. He finds a theology of God's utter vulnerability, through which creation, as much as

Christ's cross, is a poignant handing-over of a priceless gift – a pattern priestly ministry re-enacts in daily faithfulness. He perceives the invariable risk that lies at the heart of creating something new. We will never know how people or things might turn out. The experience of God is that, in the midst of the joy that exists because of the created world, there is a hidden agony: the agony that springs from the love God has for all creation. The poem became a hymn in this setting by Barry Rose.
- Grayston Ives is an English composer who sang as a tenor in the Kings Singers between 1975 and 1985. He then became Fellow and Tutor in Music at Magdalen College, Oxford until 2009. 'Listen sweet dove' was published in 2005. The lyrics are taken from a longer poem called Whitsunday by George Herbert.
- 'Hear my prayer' was composed by Felix Mendelssohn in Germany in 1844. The librettist was William Bartholomew, who also collaborated with Mendelssohn on his oratorio Elijah. It is based on Psalm 55, which portrays prayer fundamentally as a means of escape in the face of crisis. The celebrated section known popularly as 'O for the wings of a dove' gave its name to the 1902 novel by Henry James. The novel tells the story of how Millie schemes for her fiancé Merton to marry the rich but sickly Kate and inherit her fortune so she and Merton could live in comfort for the rest of their lives, and how the plan goes awry. It was rated the 26th-best English language novel of the twentieth century.

Choir: 'Morning glory, starlit sky' – Barry Rose (Cathedral Music)
Choir: 'Listen sweet dove' – Grayston Ives (RSCM)
Choir: 'O for the wings of a dove' (from 'Hear my prayer') – Felix Mendelssohn

'How great thou art'

- 'O Lord my God' was set to a Swedish traditional melody and based on a poem written by Carl Boberg in 1885. Carl Boberg and some friends were returning home to Mönsterås from Kronobäck, where they had joined an afternoon service. A thundercloud appeared on the horizon, and lightning flashed across the sky. Strong winds swept over the meadows and billowing fields of grain. The thunder pealed in loud claps. Then rain came in cool fresh showers. In a short while the storm was over, and a rainbow appeared.
- When Boberg arrived home, he beheld through the window the bay of Mönsterås like a mirror before him. From the woods on the other side of the bay, he heard the song of a thrush. The church bells were tolling in the quiet evening. This series of sights, sounds and experiences inspired the writing of the song.
- It was translated into German and then into Russian. It was finally translated into English from the Russian by English missionary Stuart K. Hine, who added two original verses of his own. The composition was set to a Russian melody.

It was popularized during the Billy Graham crusades. It was voted the UK's favourite hymn by BBC1 *Songs of Praise* viewers.

Hymn: 'O Lord my God, when I in awesome wonder' ('How great thou art')

'The Birds' Lullaby'

- Sarah Quartel is a Canadian composer and educator inspired by the life-changing relationships that can occur while making choral music. She lives in London, Ontario.
- This is an a cappella setting of words by E. Pauline Johnson. Emily Pauline Johnson, also known by her Mohawk stage name Tekahionwake, was a Canadian poet, author and performer. She was well known in the late nineteenth and early twentieth centuries. Her father was a hereditary Mohawk chief; her mother was an English immigrant. Her family originated from New York State. She was a key figure in defining Canadian literature and in modelling indigenous women's writing.

Choir: 'The Birds' Lullaby' – Sarah Quartel (OUP)

Blessings

Choir: 'A Prayer of St Patrick' – John Rutter (OUP)

Blessings

- The Old Testament notion of blessing is founded on Genesis 12, where God promises Abraham that in his descendants all nations will find a blessing. This changes the idea of blessing from a general wish for another's well-being into a commission that the other person live a life of service to others.
- The other key Old Testament text for the notion of blessing is Numbers 6, in which the Lord makes his face to shine upon the Israelites, and the result is peace. So we get a constant balance between what we could call a notion of blessing based on 'for' – what God will do for people – and a notion of blessing based on 'with' – God's face being shown to people, and people becoming the agents of God's peaceful purpose.

Robert Robinson

- Robinson was born at Swaffham, Norfolk, in 1735. He was 8 at the time of his father's death. He was a very bright, headstrong boy who, aged 14, was sent to London for an apprenticeship with a barber. Robert proceeded to get into more trouble, taking on a life of drinking and gambling. At 17, Robert and some of his drinking companions decided to attend an evangelistic meeting, with a plan to make fun of the proceedings. When George Whitefield began to preach, Robert felt as if the sermon was just for him. The words of the evangelist would haunt him for the next three years.
- In 1755, at the age of 20, Robert finally yielded his life to Christ, and very soon thereafter answered a call to the ministry. Three years later, as he was preparing to preach a sermon at the Calvinist Methodist Chapel in Norfolk, England, Robert wrote 'Come, thou fount of every blessing' to complement his sermon. It was based on 1 Samuel 7.12, in which the prophet Samuel raises a stone as a monument, saying, 'Hitherto hath the Lord helped us' (KJV).
- Thereafter, from the age of 24, Robinson spent most of his life as pastor of Stone-Yard Baptist Chapel, Cambridge.

Hymn: 'Come, thou fount of every blessing' (Nettleton)

Three anthems

- The words of 'God be in my head' date back to a French publication of 1490. The simple prayer offers a holistic path of my life, from thought to vision to perception even unto death. Of the many settings, the one by sometime Master of the King's Musick Henry Walford Davies is the best loved. It was published in 1910. Walford Davies was part of the great generation of English church music. He was organist of the Temple Church and of St George's Chapel, Windsor, and later Professor of Music at Aberystwyth. He is most associated with his hymn-singing broadcasts at the start of the war.
- Richard of Chichester was committed to restoring reverence to Catholic liturgy in the thirteenth century and rooted out priests who mumbled their way through the Mass. He was serious also about being close to those experiencing poverty: he sold his gold and silver and gave away the proceeds. He was a vegetarian, and wore a lambswool hair shirt. His famous prayer was adapted by Stephen Schwartz and John-Michael Tebelak for the song 'Day by day' for the 1971 musical *Godspell*.
- The well-known Irish benediction, here set by Bob Chilcott, was originally written in Irish Gaelic. It plays with the three elemental forces: wind, rain and sun. Each of them has powerful scriptural resonances – the wind and fire of Mount Sinai at the giving of the Ten Commandments, the wind that Elijah heard on

Mount Carmel, the rain that came upon the prophets of Baal at Elijah's behest, the sun that went dark at Christ's crucifixion. Most significantly, each of these elemental powers can give the feeling of being overwhelmed – in both terrifying and inspiring contexts.

Choir: 'God be in my head' – Henry Walford Davies (public domain, various hymn books)
Choir: 'Saint Richard's Prayer' – Joanna Forbes L'Estrange (RSCM)
Choir: 'An Irish blessing' – Bob Chilcott (OUP)

'Glory to thee, my God, this night'

- The Reformation composer Thomas Tallis composed a hymn in 1567 called 'God grant with grace'. The words that are most familiar today were written by Thomas Ken, who is best known for his influential book *A Serious Call to a Devout and Holy Life*.
- A canon is a melody that can be sung in parts. 'Glory to thee, my God, this night' is a four-line hymn that successfully translates into a canon, with each of four voices joining in at the beginning of a new line.
- Tallis was a great survivor, managing to find favour with Henry VIII, Edward VI, Mary Tudor and Elizabeth I, composing to both English and Latin texts. His influence was even greater because he controlled the way music was printed for decades.

Hymn: 'Glory to thee, my God, this night' (Tallis' Canon)

'The Lord bless you and keep you'

- John Rutter composed this setting of the Aaronic blessing from Numbers 6 in 1981 for the memorial service for Edward T. Chapman, the man who had taught him music at Highgate School in London. It was sung to celebrate the 100th birthday of the Queen Mother in 2000 and the wedding of Meghan and Harry in 2018. The blessing is often used by Jewish parents to bless their children before the Friday night Shabbat meal.

Choir: 'The Lord bless you and keep you' – John Rutter (OUP)